Louder Than Words

Louder Than Words:

Searching for Heart in a Heartless World

BRAD STEPHENS

WIPF & STOCK · Eugene, Oregon

LOUDER THAN WORDS:
Searching for Heart in a Heartless World

Copyright © 2021 Brad Stephens. All rights reserved. Except for brief quotations in critical publications or reviews, no part of this book may be reproduced in any manner without prior written permission from the publisher. Write: Permissions, Wipf and Stock Publishers, 199 W. 8th Ave., Suite 3, Eugene, OR 97401.

Wipf & Stock
An Imprint of Wipf and Stock Publishers
199 W. 8th Ave., Suite 3
Eugene, OR 97401

www.wipfandstock.com

PAPERBACK ISBN: 978-1-6667-1080-9
HARDCOVER ISBN: 978-1-6667-1081-6
EBOOK ISBN: 978-1-6667-1082-3

11/09/21

Scripture quotations are from the ESV® Bible (The Holy Bible, English Standard Version®), copyright © 2001 by Crossway Bibles, a publishing ministry of Good News Publishers. Used by permission. All rights reserved.

Excerpt from www.askntwright.com Cessationism and Why I pray in Tongues. https://www.youtube.com/watch?v=sla0T4X-I8o. Used by permission. All rights reserved.

Paideia Press works used by permission. All rights reserved.

This book is dedicated to my wife Judy.
She is a true helpmate and the love of my life.

"It is thus possible to be very much at home in the details of the Scriptures and not to know the word of God…A proper understanding of the Scriptures is only possible when we are already in the grip of the Word, the active, renewing Word of God"

— H. E. Runner

Contents

Introduction | 1

1 Fragmentation of Faith | 13
2 Fragmentation of Church | 22
3 Fragmentation of Science | 35
4 Fragmentation of Work | 50
5 Fragmentation of Philosophy | 60
6 Ignoring Fragmentation—American Pragmatism | 71
7 Fragmentation of Humanity: Part 1 | 82
8 Fragmentation of Humanity: Part 2 | 98
9 Fragmentation in Summary | 111
10 The Spirit Walk | 117
11 Pressing On | 124
12 Realizing I Am Not Alone | 128

Bibliography | 133

Introduction

THIS WORK FOCUSES ON the historical outworking of a phenomenon known as fragmentation. Life as we know it in the day-to-day is severely fragmented. That brokenness did not happen overnight, and the main section of this work is a relatively brief account of how the world began to be seen as fragmented. It will take the reader on a whirlwind trip of philosophy, science, and more philosophy that led scientists to abandon philosophy and philosophers to abandon science, at least in Europe. America, being the rebellious entity that it is, has chosen to forgo philosophy altogether, disregarding the need for foundations of any sort and claims: We built this city. However, Scripture seems to say that the works of humans apart from the grace of God are a stench in God's nose.

If what scientists, philosophers, and pragmatists believed about the world were true, then we as a people would not be able to find hope. Thankfully, there is a true foundation under the shoddy workmanship of the modern and postmodern age, which will be briefly discussed at the end of this chapter.

The latter part of this work is more personal in nature. Perhaps the best way to describe it is as a recognition of personal fragmentation that led to the acknowledgement of my need for grace. Let me qualify that by saying I am a well-loved and respected person who is of no import to the big wheels that roll toward oblivion. I find myself grateful to have stumbled into the process of finding increasing personal wholeness within the wholeness of creation regardless of who notices. Life is not anything like I thought it would be, but then nothing, absolutely nothing is. I refer to myself as of no import because in the age that I live you must have a wristband issued from the ones who dole out power if you want to be transformed into somebody. If not, then Nobody is your name.

I have put pen to paper since I can remember. It is what I do. It is what my father did. Just a couple of weeks ago (as of this writing) I found an aged scrap of paper with my father's notes scrawled on it. It was a revelation and an insight that he left to whoever would clean out one of his many toolboxes. He died in 2018. I know more about him from scraps of paper that I have found in the last couple of years, scattered randomly throughout his belongings, than a lifetime of words from his mouth ever revealed. I did not want it to be true, but I am much like my father.

I'm not sure that I have ever been able to understand my own past by looking from my present (which is as far into the future as I can get). However, I am wont to believe that by understanding the past more fully I can perhaps have a fuller, if not complete, understanding of the present. Such an approach is known as a therapeutic model of counseling. In one sense perhaps, given my background with clinical psychology, the latter part of this work is an attempt to apply a therapeutic model to the culture of my life to understand my own journey. Once again trying to find the wholeness of life within the brokenness of humanity.

What happened in the life of America that opened the doors I walked through? I may be the first person in my family to hazard that journey. I cannot think of any theologians who have attempted to tie their theological journey to their personal life. The key to answering that question, I believe, is the well-worn phrase, "Context is everything," and as I write this, I realize that I have, as a product of my times, been cut off from my context.

This segregation from the past is the culmination of a myriad of things that were outside my control. It is the result of the events that are discussed in the first section of this work. In other words, it is the way the modern, and especially the postmodern, world prefers to live.

Introduction

However, from where I am now, I understand that nothing happens in this world by itself—everything is integrally connected. Contrary to popular opinion there is a wholeness to reality. Ideas do not simply appear randomly or in isolation. They are connected to life as it is lived within the context of time. These are thoughts that are often overlooked or seen as passé in our own day and age. That does not make them wrong; for the most part it simply leaves them ignored.

I am writing this historical/philosophical/theological biography because I fully believe in the wholeness of life. I am not this or that or the other, I am all of it at once. I am this, that, and the other. I am a human being created in the image of God (whatever that means) and therefore I am meant to be a unified whole. I might have caught a glimpse of that early on, but it did not last long. I have only just begun to remember that wholeness while at the same time learning to live in it for the very first time.

My father, for all of his reading of the Bible and striving to be true to its words, could never find wholeness. In fact, his diligent reading of Scripture mixed with Dale Carnegie and the power of positive thinking were his attempts to get a wristband in this world while simultaneously hoping that if he was not granted one by the powers that be on Earth, he would have one waiting for him in heaven (from the Platonist point of view in which his generation understood the Scriptures).

If being a unified whole was the end of the story there would be nothing to write because I do not have a clue what that looks like; for in the world in which we live, the wholeness that was once the essence of creation was shattered into a billion pieces long before I was born. I like to tell my congregation that there have only been three human beings in the history of the world who have ever been truly alive and truly unbroken, in other words, whole. They are Adam and Eve (before their rebellion) and Jesus. The rest of us are the shattered, walking dead, some walking towards life and wholeness, some walking away. All of us fragmented.

In writing this, I am tracing the story of death while at the same time mapping out the slow emergence of signs of life in this dying body. I am telling the story in the way I know best—pushing thoughts and ideas until they break. My life is a story of driving ninety miles an hour down the road to the Promised Land only to crash into the wall of a dead-end street. I have picked up scars along the way and those scars remind me that I am still alive—no, more alive than I used to be—still pressing on to the higher calling of my Lord. These days I don't even try to define that call at all. It is simply life as I live it. That is a huge change in perspective for me because in the first part of my story I just wanted to leave life behind. I had plenty of theological reasons for that; whether they were sound or not is another story.

However, the story does not begin with me for the simple fact that, as I said previously, there is a wholeness to creation. I am not an island, though I spent a large part of my life pretending I was. I am rooted and grounded in a specific trajectory of history. I am an American with all the baggage that entails. My roots are in the south, but I grew up in the north. I am descended from two lines of family: Stephens and Finney, English and Scotch-Irish. None of that is irrelevant to who I am or how my life unfolded.

This is not a neutral tale. I write from what I would call a Reformational perspective rooted in obscure thinkers like Herman Dooyeweerd, H. Evan Runner, and John Vandersteldt, among others. I see truth because there is a singular reality, but it is not the reality posited by either side of the Enlightenment coin of thought—Rationalism or Romanticism. Nor is it that of the free-for-all that is postmodernity. Going against the grain even further, the ground upon which I place my feet is not that which is posited by most who would call themselves Christians in the western world, though it is thoroughly rooted in the life, death, and resurrection of the man named Jesus.

The title of the book—*Louder Than Words*—comes from the final song on the final Pink Floyd album, *The Endless River*. It is also the second part of the well-known phrase, "Actions speak louder than words." That phrase is an integral part of how I understand the world. I like to rephrase it and say: We do what we believe to be true.

Introduction

It is my prayer that should you accept the mission to read this experiment in both writing and thinking. It will be a step towards verifying the validity of that statement. The remainder of this chapter is intended to give you a foundation from which to understand how both the history of the modern and postmodern eras unfolded and the biblical response to that unfolding.

Let me stress once again: These words I am putting to paper are in no way neutral. What I am writing is 100 percent biased. There is nothing I can do about that except be honest. This notion really took hold of me in 2018 when my father died. The comments that I heard, the notes left on his obituary page, blew my mind because I did not recognize the man they were talking about. Their experience of reality was not my experience of reality.

In seeing that, I finally began to understand the depth of meaning encapsulated in the concept of the whole truth. I realized that to understand who my father was one must see the various perspectives all at once: His own perspective, my mother's perspective, his parents, his children and grandchildren, brothers and sisters, friends from every era of his life. Everyone that ever knew him, knew him from their own perspective. Why? Because every perspective reveals a part of the wholeness that was and is my father. All of what I have just written is equally true about myself. My perspective of me is incomplete. Through the years, as I have made amends to people I have hurt, I have been surprised that their perspectives of the same events were nothing like mine.

My point in all of this is that what I am writing is not the whole truth. It is the truth from my limited perspective, and it is reflected to you through the brokenness that is my life. In saying that I am not embracing relativism. Rather, I am aware that the creation in which we live is the Creator's truth. The Creator alone can see all the perspectives at the same time. He sees the complete wholeness and the brokenness of the created universe—the created, however, can only see the whole from their limited perspective. The fact that individuals see the same thing from different perspectives simply reveals our limitations as created beings.

At the same time, it also reveals the unity of the creation. For example, no one who knew my father would ever suggest that he did not exist. That would be absurd. Too often, everyday experience is written off by the powers that be as of no import. In the age that we live some go so far as to say that we cannot really know the world around us. Yet, they continue to live their ordinary lives: They go to the bathroom, they eat, and they try to communicate to their peers.

It is important we understand that everyday experience is real. The world in which we live *is* meaning. Even if there were no humans, the creation would still be full of meaning because it was created to be meaning-full in every aspect of its being.[1] Creation is a whole, a totality, in which we are included.[2] But more than that: the creation is good.

The presuppositions with which I now write have not always been a part of my life. As I noted earlier, they are deeply rooted in what is known as a Reformational point of view of the world which grew out of the philosophical work of Herman Dooyeweerd and H. Evan Runner amongst others.[3] That which follows in this introduction is an incomplete list of the presuppositions that help me understand the world in which I live and move and have my being better than anything else I have ever embraced. It is far from complete, but it includes my main foundational supports.

My Building Blocks

First, I understand that the world in which we live was created by the one true God, who is outside of and set apart from creation. Creation includes everything within what is known as the time-space continuum. Second, the creation was created to be good, and in fact, it has always been and always will be very good.

---

1. Troost, *Reformational Philosophy*, 75.
2. Spier, *Introduction to Christian Philosophy*, 12.
3. See bibliography for an extended list of influential Reformational books.

Introduction

A side note here about creation, it is important to understand that when Gen 1:1 says, "In the beginning God created the heavens and the earth," it is not referring to sky and space and Earth and the other planets. Those words are referring to two separate but connected spheres of the created universe. The Earth was created for humans and the heavens were created to be the abode of other spiritual beings such as angels, demons, principalities and powers. It is also in this place that the resurrected human Jesus, the ruler of both Heaven and Earth, abides until the rebellion of humanity, induced by rebellious principalities and powers, has been dealt with once and for all.

My point in saying this is to make it clear that both Heaven and Earth are a part of the created universe. The heavens and all the non-human beings that abide there are a part of the created universe. They are not super- or supra-natural. God alone is supranatural. He alone can be outside of time and space. We cannot experience our Creator at all unless he comes down to our level and reveals his ways by dumbing down his works so that they can be experienced at the creational level.[4]

Earthly human beings and heavenly beings cannot experience anything that is beyond or above creation. We are all a part, and will always be a part, of the created order. No part of God's created order can directly experience anything that is outside the created order. In other words, no one in heaven or on Earth can experience God in his essence. That is why God must condescend, come down to our level and to the level of angels in order to interact with his creation. We are made to experience life within creation and so are angels and demons. God makes accommodations so that he can have a relationship with his creation.

Getting back to point three: Humanity was created in the image of God, both male and female, equal in standing and authority before God, to be his viceregents over the creation with the aim of transforming the entire planet into a garden that was fully developed. Another way of saying it is that the first humans were called

---

4. Wolters, *Creation Regained*, 11, 87–88.

to advance the kingdom of God over the entire planet as God's stewards.

However, there was a snafu. God created the first humans in freedom. They were not robots, nor were they autonomous. They were beings created to advance God's kingdom and fellowship with him in the good world. Though they were free to walk with God in the cool of the day, they were also free to turn their backs on God and rebel against him.

It is important to note that humans have always been and will always be free to choose, but the freedom to choose is not the same thing as being autonomous. Human beings cannot be autonomous, self-determining, because they are not self-made—they are created. They were created with the ability to walk in life and wholeness.

The key to that last sentence is "wholeness." Certainly, the structure of the creation is still whole and still good, yet something has happened which keeps humans from experiencing wholeness within that totality. That something was rebellion against life. Why would the Creator of a very good universe take the risk of having it all go awry? Because God values freedom over goodness. He did not create slaves, he created fully functioning human beings who were meant to reflect his image in the created world. They were meant to expand the kingdom of the Creator over the entire globe by lovingly and carefully expanding the garden in which they had been placed until it covered the entire Earth.

Mutiny on the Bounty

Enter the dragon. His first words to humanity were the first lies they ever heard. They knew nothing of deceit and so when they heard the words, they believed them. The result was a mutiny against life itself and the end of life as they had known it. Too often in this tale the woman gets the blame. Yet the woman was the one who was deceived. The man was not deceived. Instead, he walked purposely and willfully into death.

Introduction

The history of the world, as we read about it in history books, is the outflow of the broken mess of humanity's rebellion against the good God. It is a story of war and death, progress and collapse, arrogance and humiliation. It is the story of alienation and brokenness. It is the consequence of human choices.

As soon as the humans rebelled, consequences followed. The Earth was cursed to make it harder for those who rebelled, resulting in thorns, weeds, disease, fear in animals, miscommunication, and family discord. Work became more difficult. Death entered the scene for the first time. All the mess that we see, with death and dysfunction being just an ordinary part of our lives, began there.

It seems to me that this thing called death was more than just physical death. I believe that in some sense we died to the creation as it was. We could no longer see the world as it originally existed. Perhaps it was like watching the Wizard of Oz backwards: The picture started in full color and when we rebelled everything turned to differing shades of gray.

Human beings have no idea what the creation looked like when it was whole because our eyes and our senses have lost the capacity to see reality in its true essence. We are only guessing at what wholeness entails, for we have no example—except Jesus—and our information about him is quite limited. We are blind to the wholeness of reality. We only know the curse. Thankfully, even though the world is cursed to us, it is still an amazingly wonderful place despite the corruptness we have begotten. We also have the promise of restoration.

The rebellion of humanity was not a surprise to the Creator, nor did it disrupt his plan to develop his kingdom in the material universe. One important point that is often left out of some versions of this story, is that even though the world is cursed it is still very good. Except for human beings, the earthly creation remains obedient to its creational intent. Even as it obeys the command to be cursed, it is still very good, because it is doing what the Creator asked of it.

Hope for a Hopeless Mess

Up to the point of mutiny, humans were the rulers of the Earth, the image of God to the world. When they rebelled, Satan became the ruler of this world. Yet to this usurper the Creator made a promise: "I will put enmity between you and the woman, and between your offspring and her offspring; he shall bruise your head, and you shall bruise his heel."[5]

That statement is rather oblique. In fact, it was meant to be. Paul, at the end of the book of Romans, tells us that this promise was a mystery that was kept secret for long ages. Why? Because, as he tells us in 1 Cor 2:8, if the rulers of this age, the principalities and powers that usurped humanity's authority, had understood what had to happen to restore authority to human beings they would not have crucified the Lord of glory.

The unfolding of the history of Israel in the Old Testament, their early successes and their ultimate failure, was for a single purpose which was to demonstrate that the rebellious human race could not save itself from the mess into which it willfully entered. They could not transform their hard hearts into hearts of flesh. They could not circumcise their own hearts. Their only hope was for God to intervene.

Adam Again

Enter the one who would crush the head of the dragon. Jesus of Nazareth was conceived in the womb of Mary by the Holy Spirit. This conception was not of Mary's egg or of Joseph's seed. It was an act of God in the created world. This was necessary because the child was to be the new Adam. He was created by God in the womb of Mary, born into this Dark Age, and by the grace of God he learned obedience through suffering. His short time on this Earth was a process of circumcising his heart.

The struggle of dying to himself was culminated in the Garden of Gethsemane where in agony he cried out to God: "If there

---

5. Gen 3:15.

Introduction

is any other way to do your will, please do it" as he sweat drops of blood. There was not another way. And so, he resigned himself to willingly die, trusting that God would be faithful to his word. He hung on the cross and with his last words he said, "It is finished." At that point, the circumcision of his heart was complete. The second Adam walked faithfully with God even though it cost him his life. Because of that, God raised him from the dead.

The resurrection from the dead is the evidence that Jesus is the firstborn of a new creation. He now sits in created heaven ruling and reigning over both heaven and Earth. He is Lord of all. Any who are willing to die to themselves and have their own hearts circumcised are welcome into the new creation. Jesus will reign until all his enemies are put under his feet. The kingdom of God has come to Earth but not in its fullness. The war still goes on between darkness and light, but things have significantly changed in the created realm of the principalities and powers.

The question for me is: Why does this whole rebellion aspect of creation need to go on so long? I do not have an answer, but I am beginning to understand that time is an essential part of the created order. It is not some add on. It is not something you can bend or move like Dr. Who does. Time, number, space, and motion are not objects that can be bent and stretched and turned back on one another.

Herman Dooyeweerd in his work, *A New Critique of Theoretical Thought*, laid out what is known as the modal aspects of creaturely reality. Time is the base in which all of the modes operate. Without time creation cannot be. It is not simply a construct that is used for our convenience. However, to describe the modal aspects, we must look at the various parts separately. They do not act independently, nor were they created to be independent. The modes of creation act as a whole and they appeared, as a whole, when God spoke them into existence.

In the midst of time, number appears (not numerals but individual different things), one second follows another. But for one second to follow another there must be space in which individual seconds can exist; within space there must be motion in order to get from one point to the next. Dooyeweerd continues to expand these modes of being but this will suffice for our purposes.[6]

All of the modes of being are connected in reciprocal ways, they point forward, and they point backward and give continuous feedback. It is this continual interconnectedness that makes up the meaningfulness of created reality. The individual aspects of created reality work together simultaneously and unceasingly, as a unified whole, and in doing so the creation comes to fruition.

This is a short summary of the major presuppositions that I hold concerning the world in which I live. It is not the story or the journey of my life, but it is the foundation for how I now make sense of this jumble of experiences that I call my life, so far. What follows is the story, the narrative, of how I came to believe in the goodness of created reality and the one who created it.

---

6. Dooyeweerd, *New Critique*, vol. 1. See also Troost, *Reformational Philosophy*; Kalsbeek, *Contours of a Christian Philosophy*; Spier, *Introduction to Christian Philosophy*.

1

Fragmentation of Faith

WITHOUT FAITH THERE WOULD be no America. That may sound odd given the dominant secular foundation of the twenty-first century where we divide faith and religion from things that can be measured. From that scientific perspective, faith and religion belong in the category of things that are not worthy of study or conversation. For, scientifically, if something cannot be measured it is of no import. Such a presupposition, when looked at with limited bias, is found to be blatantly false.

Let's begin with a simple question: How do human beings become alive? I am not talking about sperm and eggs and rock and roll; I am talking about life. You see, no one knows *how* a human being comes to life. We only know that they do. We do not even know what life is. We only know what it is not. The same is true with all other living things. Yet we do not have to stop there; we can go back to the entire material universe—where did it come from? No one knows.

There are many grand theories, but theories are not fact. In the twenty-first century the most predominant answer to this singular question is to simply ignore it while increasing the volume of our voices as we espouse our theories, as if ignorance or volume can turn theory into fact. The truth is when it comes to such matters, everyone believes their theory by faith.

With regard to where and how we live there are two opposing positions of faith. The most predominant position of faith in western culture is that the material world is meaningless—one big accident. The next most prominent position of faith is that the world was created with meaning to be meaningful. It simply *is* meaning. These two theories are mutually exclusive, though throughout the ages people on both sides of the issue have tried to create a hybrid. But no one has been able to determine whether that hybrid should be called "meaningless meaning" or "meaningful meaninglessness." If faith is the foundation of religion then, given the above statements, all of life is religious.[1]

This work that you are reading is a work of faith. By faith, I believe that I can find meaning and understanding in the present by looking at the past. But to understand my past I need some inkling of where I came from. I have finally come to understand that history is the story of connected meaning, though as a child I was told by example and words that history was irrelevant. "You have got to leave the past behind and embrace the future." But if you leave the past behind, and I write this from experience, you find yourself adrift on the waves of hap and circumstance. The result is that you find yourself with no direction home.

When one thinks of the founding of America the notion of the Puritans more than likely comes to mind, as well it should. But before we examine the development of Puritan religion and the fragmentation of Protestantism, we need to first examine the shifts in thinking that opened the door to the Protestant Reformation in the first place.

A Brief History of the Development of Christianity

Before the Protestant Reformation the Catholic Church was the sole authority of western culture. Yet that did not happen overnight,

---

1. Runner, *Walking in the Way*, 2: 181–82.

nor was it as simple as an outworking of the Christian notion of the kingdom of God taking dominion over the Earth. In fact, Arthur Lovejoy, in his work *The Great Chain of Being*, puts forth the idea that western culture began as the struggle between two gods, or rather two conflicting personalities of God in the mind of Plato. He writes: "These two were, indeed, identified as one being with two aspects. But the ideas corresponding to the 'aspects' were ideas of two antithetical kinds of being."[2]

The first god to develop in Greek culture was that of continual change. It was the "deification of a formless, cyclical stream of life" out of which "emerged the individual forms of plant, animal and human being, which then matured, perished, and came to life again."[3] This god continually produced life, ever changing life, with a diversity of creatures and the continual material evolution of nature in time with unending change.

The other god was "the absolute of otherworldliness—self-sufficient, out of time, alien to the categories of human thought and experience, needing no world of lesser beings to supplement or enhance its own eternal self-contained perfection."[4] One could also add "changeless" and "static" to those descriptors of the second half of the split-personality-god of Plato. For the Greeks, the history of the world was the eternal struggle between these two aspects of god. Herman Dooyeweerd classifies this conflict found in Greek culture as the dialectical struggle between form and matter.[5]

Christianity was birthed in a culture that had fully embraced the Greek ideal. For two hundred years the battle between these ideals was intense. However, by the fourth century the two world views began to be synthesized into something new. Lovejoy notes that "Two men more than any others determined the formula for this new compound of old ingredients."[6] They were the fourth-century Christian convert from Neoplatonism, Augustine, and

---

2. Lovejoy, *Great Chain of Being*, 315.
3. Lovejoy, *Great Chain of Being*, 315.
4. Lovejoy, *Great Chain of Being*, 315.
5. Dooyeweerd, *Roots of Western Culture*, 15–22.
6. Lovejoy, *Great Chain of Being*, 67.

Dionysius, the convert of St. Paul whose letter to the church was discovered in the fifth century. (The latter is now known to be a fraudulent document known as Pseudo-Dionysius but unfortunately that was not discovered until the fifteenth century).

Over the next century this synthesis continued to be defined. It was not until the thirteenth century that Thomas Aquinas put the capstone on the synthesis of Greek and Christian thought. Thomas took the works of Augustine and Pseudo-Dionysius, as well as ideas from Neoplatonism, mixed them with Muslim translations/interpretations of the Greeks (for example, Averroes and Avicenna), and synthesized them with Christianity. In the process, the Greek dialectical struggle of form and matter was transformed into a new dialectical struggle that became known as nature and grace. The theological support system that accompanied this shift became known as Roman Catholic scholasticism.

This is important because it completely changed the foundation of Christianity by replacing the God revealed in the Bible with the god of Plato and Aristotle. "In the Medieval view ancient paganism was preserved as a distinct area or sphere unreformed by biblical revelation, the so-called realm of Nature (and Natural Reason). To it was added the area of special revelation, of grace and faith, the so-called realm of Grace."[7] From this perspective Nature, seen through the eyes of Greek philosophy, remained a natural light. To that is added the light of special revelation.

It is essential to note that at the root of this concept of nature/grace the natural light of reason is considered to be autonomous—it exists apart from the revelation of God. Natural reason then becomes the interpreter of the sphere of grace. This "was the underlying governing motive of thinkers in Christian circles for centuries, and even the reformation, from the beginning, failed to overcome it."[8]

One of the most impactful ideas to come out of this was a new and unbiblical understanding of both God and creation known as the great chain of being. This notion was such a foundational part

---

7. Runner, *Walking in the Way*, 2:212.
8. Runner, *Walking in the Way*, 2:212.

Fragmentation of Faith

of scholasticism that it was equally held to be true by Catholics and Protestants, proponents of the Enlightenment and Romanticism, Puritans, Anabaptists, and heretics alike. To understand the history of the western world one must understand the great chain of being.

Simply put, the great chain of being is a view of how reality works that is loosely tied to the Greek philosopher Plato and his concept that all material things are a reflection of the eternal non-changing forms in the eternal other world. It was Plotinus the Neoplatonist (205–27 CE) who systematized the concept.

The Encyclopedia Britannica summarizes the main points of this system of belief very well:

> The term denotes three general features of the universe, plentitude, continuity, and graduation. The principle of plentitude states that the universe is fully exhibiting the maximum diversity of kinds of existences; everything possible (i.e., non-self-contradictory) is actual. The principle of continuity asserts that the universe is composed of an infinite series of forms, each of which shares with its neighbor at least one attribute. According to the principle of linear graduation, the series ranges in hierarchical order from the barest type of existence to the *ens perfectissimium*, or God.[9]

In other words, everything begins with God and emanates out of God in a descending hierarchy with each step downward being less holy and less like God. Ultimately, in this view there is a oneness that is similar to Eastern thought in that everything is ultimately God with decreasing levels of holiness. Humanity finds its place in the middle of that hierarchy—the middle link between holiness and non-holy: a hybrid of spiritual and material.[10] What follows is the history of the development of that hierarchy within those who have human form.

A second idea that is inherent in the scholasticism of Thomas is that of autonomous natural reason. If natural reason is

---

9. "Great Chain of Being," *Encyclopedia Britanica*.
10. Lovejoy, *Great Chain of Being*, 190.

autonomous over God and humans, then revelation, in a biblical sense, becomes meaningless. Reason, which is equally available to all, can reasonably be used to create a different, even a better, understanding of how the world works than that of revelation. Who is to say which is right? Since all have access to this independent, autonomous reason then every man and god can do what is right in their own eyes; they only need to be assured that it is reasonable. Thus, the door was opened for a struggle for authority.

Welcome to Struggleville

And struggle is exactly what came about. Early in the fourteenth century the great synthesis of nature and grace began to show signs of deterioration beginning with the philosophical work of the Franciscan monk William of Occam (1287–1337). His work announced for the first time that there could be no point of contact between the realm of nature and the realm of grace because of the inner dualism inherent in the foundational ground-motive of nature and grace. He clearly understood that there could be no reconciliation between the Greek understanding of nature and that of Christianity. If Christianity were true, there could not be multiple eternal foundations of creation—the Scriptures demanded one sovereign and eternal Creator who created all things.

"However, in order to break with the Greek deification of reason [Occam] ended up in another extreme. He interpreted the will of the divine creator as despotic arbitrariness. . .We may say that Occam deprived the law of its intrinsic value."[11] For him, God was not bound by anything—he was completely free to do as he pleased. Law only applied to "the sinful world of nature."[12] Such a view brought forth uncertainty about the faithfulness of God. If he was not obligated to the law what would stop him from changing his will as circumstances changed?

---

11. Dooyeweerd, *Roots of Western Culture*, 138.
12. Dooyeweerd, *Roots of Western Culture*, 138.

Fragmentation of Faith

Occam's nominalism revealed the vulnerability of the nature-grace ground-motive. The supposed synthesis between Greek and Christian thought had been destroyed in the opinion of many. What could be done? The options were slim. One could return to the Christian ground-motive of creation-fall-redemption or one could build upon nature alone—now that all contact between nature and grace was deemed impossible. The first option led to the Reformation. The second led to the modern concept of reality based upon the autonomy of human reason.

Obviously, both paths were taken but in each instance the grip of the old ground-motive of nature and grace was slow to let go.

The Reformation

The strength of the grip of the nature-grace ground motive can be seen in the work of Martin Luther (1483–1546) who was schooled in the teaching of Occam. Certainly, the old foundational beliefs of Aquinas were altered by the influence of Occam, but they were not eliminated. The church still sought a synthesis of nature and grace; Occam had sought a separation of the two. Luther longed to see nature swallowed up by grace. He saw a sharp divide between nature and grace and under the influence of Occam's nominalism this divide was worked out as the struggle between law and gospel. In keeping with Occam, Luther saw the law as confined to the sinful world of nature. However, when a sinner comes to repentance and is saved by grace through faith alone, he is saved from the law and in fact placed above the law. Salvation frees the Christian "not only from the judgment of the law, which sin brought upon us, but in the life of grace the Christian is free from the law itself, standing entirely above the law."[13]

Yet the Christian still must live in the natural world. From Luther's perspective redemption prepared the way for the death of nature, not its restoration from the fall. In the interim it was

---

13. Dooyeweerd, *Roots of Western Culture*, 140.

"God's will that Christians subject themselves to the ordinances of earthly life."[14] Fleeing the world was not an option for Luther; one must patiently endure this earthly life looking forward to the time when grace would conquer all and the natural would be subsumed by grace.

This altered form of the nature-grace ground-motive eventually evolved into Protestant scholasticism or a Protestant version of the Roman Catholic nature-grace dialectic. "The peculiar dialectic of the nature/grace ground-motive led Luther's learned friend and co-worker Melanchthon (1497–1560) to attempt a new synthesis between the Christian religion and the spirit of Greek culture."[15] In doing so, he retained the dualistic conceptions of natural versus spiritual and body versus soul.

The other major player in the Protestant Reformation was John Calvin, whose work shows a tendency to move away from the Greek synthesis of scholasticism. However, after his death, Theodore Beza took over the teaching duties of Calvin as head of the Geneva Academy. While the work of Beza in establishing the Reformed churches should not be minimized it needs to be noted that he "was an Aristotelian in his theological method, and he contributed in a very important way to the development of Aristotelian philosophical structures in the scholastic Reformed theology of the seventeenth century."[16]

The problem with the Protestant version of nature-grace was the diminished authority which confronted the new mode of religion. Before the reformation the artificial synthesis between nature and grace was held together by the absolute authority of the church which was willing to back its authority with power. As the disintegration of that unity began to develop the Roman church's attack on heresy intensified, eventually leading to the dreaded Inquisition.

In essence, in spite of the split between the Protestants and Catholics, both sides continued to view the world based on

---

14. Dooyeweerd, *Roots of Western Culture*, 141.
15. Dooyeweerd, *Roots of Western Culture*, 141
16. Runner, *Walking, vol. 2*, 600–601.

a foundation of Greek philosophy through which the Bible was interpreted. Autonomous natural reason was to be the final arbitrator in the church (and the rest of society) until the middle of the nineteenth century. For the new Protestant church there was no central established authority. Yes, the Bible was declared to be its authority but before the Reformation was out of its infancy there were already differences of opinion about what the words of Scripture meant. The authoritative word of God interpreted by autonomous reason through humans, who increasingly saw themselves as autonomous in their own right, gave birth to a new type of Tower of Babel with no group being able to communicate to or be understood by other groups. The monolith once known as Christendom held together by the authority of the Roman Church has been splintering ever since. As of 2001 there were thirty thousand different denominations worldwide.[17]

The fragmentation of authority began with the Protestant Reformation. The first division began to be seen in the sixteenth century with the rise of the Anabaptists over the issue of baptism. The Protestant reformers were no less harsh in dealing with what they considered heresy than the Catholics and by the early seventeenth century the Anabaptists were being put to death by both groups.[18] The autonomy of reason led to another major split in Protestantism over the issues of the sovereignty of God versus the free will of human beings. The issue has not and will never be resolved as long as reason is the foundation of the argument; for both concepts are equally espoused in the Scriptures though reason declares them to be irreconcilable. These two issues were simply the first in a long string of divisions caused by "rightly dividing the word of God" aided by the light of natural reason.

---

17. Barrett et al., *World Christian Encyclopedia*, 2001.
18. Estep, *Anabaptist Story*, 57.

2

Fragmentation of Church

WITH REGARD TO THE development of the church on the American continent, Protestantism was the dominant force and, for the most part, the single authoritative voice was that of scholastic Calvinism, at least in the beginning. Early on the Puritans with their congregational form of government dominated but in 1717–18 the Scotch Irish Presbyterians from Ulster began to immigrate. By 1775 over two hundred thousand Scotch Irish had come to America. As a result, Presbyterianism "grew more rapidly than any other colonial religious body in the two generations immediately preceding the Revolution."[1] By the time of the Revolution, "the two religious bodies which had the largest membership and consequently the most widespread influence throughout the colonies in the Revolutionary era were the Congregationalists and the Presbyterians."[2] The only differences between the two, at the time, were with regard to church government. Therefore, the Calvinism of the Westminster Confession, not necessarily of John Calvin, ruled supreme in the new world.[3]

1. Sweet, *Religion in the Development*, 3.
2. Sweet, *Religion in the Development*, 3.
3. Winthrop, *Religion in America*, 15.

Fragmentation of Church

The loss of a central authority over the church was keenly in evidence in the founding of the American colonies. "The necessities and the opportunities of life in the New World introduced changes of emphasis and modifications of practice. Faced with the task of beginning anew, the leaders of the churches found themselves far more dependent upon the laity than had hitherto been true, and they were forced to concede to the laity far greater powers than laity had previously enjoyed."[4] When the laity began to taste authoritative power for the first time, the door to the struggle for independence—not only religiously but also politically (and every other area of life)—was thrown wide open.

The Great Awakening

By the mid-seventeenth century, though, there was a strong Protestant religious foundation in the early colonies, "most of the people belonged to no church at all. It was not until the Great Awakening, when America experienced its 'national conversion' that this situation began to change."[5]

Richard Bushman notes that "the need for an Awakening to heal society as well as to save men's souls was widely acknowledged."[6] For eighty years prior to the 1730s "the clergy had deplored the declension of piety."[7] However, in 1734, at a Congregational church in Hampton, Massachusetts, Jonathan Edwards began a new sermon series on justification by faith, using as his text Rom 4:5: "But to him that worketh not, but believeth on him that justifieth the ungodly, his faith is counted for righteousness." After reading the text Edwards went on to proclaim, "When it is said that God justifies the ungodly, it is absurd to suppose that our godliness, taken as some goodness in us, is the ground of our justification as when it said that Christ gave sight to the blind to

---

4. Winthrop, *Religion in America*, 18.
5. Winthrop, *Religion in America*, 59.
6. Bushman, *Great Awakening*, 488.
7. Bushman, *Great Awakening*, 488.

suppose that sight was prior to, and ground of, that act of mercy in Christ.[8]

Those words laid the groundwork for the further weakening of an overarching authority in both church and state in colonial American society. They rebuked the gentry for trusting in their good and prosperous work, standing in society and wealth, while at the same time offered hope to the hopeless and those who were continually told they were worthless, no good and could not possibly change because of their idleness. The revelation was revolutionary: Goodness is not inherent in man regardless of status. Goodness—justification before God—is a gift to the ungodly who humble themselves before God, not by works, but by faith.

For some reason, this staple doctrine of the Reformation had fallen out of fashion—due perhaps to Enlightenment philosophy that was beginning to toy with the notion of the natural goodness of mankind. But these words, spoken without passion or persuasion, pierced the hearts of the people that day and began a transformation of America. In spite of his lack of presentation, style and outward zeal, while Edwards was preaching the Holy Spirit began to work on people's hearts—a revival began.

Though it was desperately needed, the revival was also radically different than anything the church had ever seen on a broad scale since the Reformation. It was emotional but that emotion was not coerced. People, with no instigation on the part of Edwards, would begin to cry out with screams and screeching, tears flowed like rivers, some fell to the ground and convulsed. It started as a trickle but soon around thirty people a week were being converted—without any altar calls or appeals for repentance on the part of Edwards. This continued for nearly two years. The flood gates were opened and a change in the church was beginning.

Over and over again for the next five years the entire population heard more and more lay preachers (whose authority came from God through natural reason) proclaiming justification by faith and along with that, the underlying theme of the equality of all mankind before God.

8. Edwards, *Justification by Faith Alone*, 10.

Fragmentation of Church

Everyone is born dead in sin. No one is born good. All must kneel before God in humbleness if they want to be righteous in God's eyes. The notion of a hierarchy of human beings as understood by the great chain of being was beginning to be examined; at least when it came to the question of economic and political standing (race was another matter).

During this same time period, John Wesley found himself failing as a minister of the Anglican Church in Savannah, Georgia and decided to return to England. On his arrival he gathered with a group called the "holy club," which he had previously formed with his brother Charles, for a meeting on Aldersgate Street in London. While Wesley was in America, revival had already begun within the "holy club" through a man named George Whitefield. Whitefield had wanted to go to Savannah to minister with Wesley, but his voyage had been delayed. In the interim he began preaching around London. The result was that everywhere he spoke it seemed that revival came.

In 1739, Whitefield left England for his first preaching tour of America. Revival broke out there just has it had in England; only the crowds were more responsive. He spoke in all thirteen colonies. It is estimated that "about 80 percent of all American colonists heard him preach at least once." At his last speaking stop there were 23,000 people present.[9] It is here that we can mark the beginning of the end of the Great Awakening.

Both revivals were similar in nature with regard to their radical change in the outworking of religion. By the end of 1741 this "new light" of revival began to elicit cries of opposition from the staunch defenders of the "old light," the guardians of the status quo. By 1742 itinerate preaching began to be outlawed in some municipalities. In spite of that, itinerate preaching only increased. It is here that the American struggle with authority within the notion of the autonomy of reason can clearly be seen. It is this struggle with religious authority that truly paves the way for the political struggle that was to follow.

---

9. Miller, "*George Whitefield.*"

The first Great Awakening is often cited as one of the causes of the American Revolution. However, the spiritual effects of that renewal, though needed, dissipated long before the revolution. By 1743 the revival began to wane. When Whitefield returned for another preaching tour in 1744, he found that most of the mainline pulpits were closed to him. Even Jonathan Edwards was quoted as saying: "The work is put to a stop everywhere, and it is a day of the Enemy's triumph.[10]

Highs and Lows

The lasting impact of the Great Awakening was to be found not in a deeper religious fervor but in the strengthening of individual authority over against authority based upon tradition. The trends in that direction can be seen in the prominence of Congregationalism which gave the local congregation authority over the pastor. "Even when ministers wanted to tighten disciplinary procedures, few congregations were willing to accept the rigorous standards implicit in the preaching of their pastors. The most shocking evidence of this fact was the callous ejection of Jonathan Edwards from his Northampton church in 1750 when he insisted upon some evidence of a personal religious experience as a prerequisite to church membership."[11]

The Great Awakening opened the door for the great breakening as the churches were split between old light and new light, established churches and new congregations being started by itinerate preachers. Soon some congregational churches were distinguishing themselves as "separate." The next step was to become Baptist and quite a number of churches did just that, especially in New England.[12]

Though the increase in numbers of church members in all denominations was large as an effect of the Great Awakening, "the

---

10. Dwight, *Biography of Jonathan Edwards*, loc. 3307.
11. Winthrop, *Religion in America*, 75.
12. Winthrop, *Religion in America*, 75.

struggle of minister against minister undermined ministerial authority at a time when a stress upon a self-authenticating religious experience was freeing the individual from dependence upon clerical opinion."[13]

The Second Great Awakening

In the 1790s and into the nineteenth century revival once again broke out in America. "The new revivalism was markedly different from the revivalism of the first awakening under Jonathan Edwards when the outpouring of God's spirit was regarded as a by-product of the faithful preaching of God's Word. Christians "waited" for these earlier revivals."[14] With the Second Awakening there was to be no waiting for the Spirit. The change reflected a subtle shift from Christianity rooted primarily in scholastic Calvinism and the sovereignty of God to a more Arminian position which developed from the strong Methodist influence found in the Whitefield revival.

The location of authority had once again been modified. No longer would revival be built upon waiting for God the Spirit to manifest his presence according to his will. It was now clear that God was waiting for humans to take the lead and provoke God to work in the lives of people. Preaching became the art of persuading people's minds instead of waiting on God to change their hearts. It was a subtle but radical shift. From this point on in America, one's relationship with God slowly became dependent on what one knew to be true and not upon the condition of the heart. Certainly, there were cries for the hearts of the people to be stirred but these were cries for emotions to come to the forefront.

In the previous awakening the emotions followed being pierced to the heart by the conviction of the word of God. In the second, the environment was manipulated to bring about feelings which opened the door for the move of God. The shift in the

---

13. Winthrop, *Religion in America*, 75.
14. Winthrop, *Religion in America*, 135.

locus of authority in this event is first, away from God through the preacher, to the individual. No longer is the minister the source of authority with regard to salvation. From this point on the individual's autonomous natural reason becomes the ultimate source of authority. A new phrase began to be spoken that had rarely been spoken in the history of Christianity: This is what I think the Scriptures mean.

With the coming of the Second Great Awakening the unified religion of the church began to increasingly become fragmented, and by the 1850s nearly twenty different denominations were formed with each having their unique spin on what the notion of "rightly dividing the word of God" meant. The word of God was certainly being divided but in a way that led to the fragmentation of the kingdom of God into multiple competing kingdoms of men.

Aftermath

With the coming of the Second Great Awakening, towards the beginning of the nineteenth century, the number of differing types of "Christianity" began to explode. It is important to note that before the Second Awakening "there was a pluralism of religious bodies, denominations, churches. But most of these had a common understanding of the Christian faith; an understanding that, under the impact of the Awakening, came to be known as 'evangelical' religion. In addition to the common faith of the churches, there was also a 'general' religion that was not pluralistic; a 'civic' religion of most people; a 'religion of the republic' with its own beliefs . . . ceremonies and . . . own days of thanksgiving existed side by side."[15]

Somehow, despite a multiplicity of perceptions on what it meant to be a Christian "the evangelical religion of the first third of the nineteenth century bred a spirit of unity that was expressed both in the revivals of the period and in the activities of the volunteer societies."[16] For some it was a move away from the church

---

15. Winthrop, *Religion in America*, 111.
16. Winthrop, *Religion in America*, 155.

Fragmentation of Church

toward the nation and the non-sectarian "religion of the republic." For others it was a move to a broader notion of what Christianity should and could be, a turn away from the technicalities of theology toward a kinder gentler move of God through his people.

In this mainline movement, sectarianism began to be seen as the surest way to quench a revival and simultaneously a barrier to the progress of the new nation. In all of this, the move away from the orthodox Calvinism of the Puritans began in earnest. Slowly both the method of the Wesley brothers and their embrace of Arminianism with its focus on the individual, began to come to the forefront in American religion. Yet the notion of sovereignty was not being eliminated from the culture—it was being transformed. Slowly, the Calvinist notion of the sovereignty of God was being replaced with the sovereignty of natural law which eventually morphed into the sovereignty of history. God was becoming an impersonal thing, a process, and a destination, and by 1839 it had begun to be spoken of as manifest destiny.

By the end of the nineteenth century Calvinist Orthodoxy would become the minority opinion in the American church and the sovereignty of both law and history would begin to be relegated to the sovereignty of chance. But at the beginning of the nineteenth century, it is probably "safe to say that even many of those who were theologically orthodox adopted a world view that in effect had Deist tendencies. They viewed the universe as a machine run by natural laws, and in practice distanced the Creator from their understanding of the everyday operations of creation. They also made a sharper distinction between the natural and supernatural."[17]

In effect, by this time, the underlying dualistic foundation of scholasticism had worked its way fully into Protestant America. "By the end of the eighteenth-century American Protestantism of almost all sorts had adopted this two-tiered world view, founded upon an empiricist epistemology, with the laws of nature below, supporting supernatural belief above . . . in which the realism of

---

17. Marsden, *Understanding Fundamentalism*, 130.

science and faith could not conflict."[18] Though it had the form of Christianity it was deeply rooted in the form-matter dialectic of the Greeks and starting to move toward the nature-freedom dialectic of modernism. The seeds of secularism inherent in the scholastic dualism of reality were beginning to grow.

In many ways this religious development was nothing but the continued outworking of the basic ideas associated with the great chain of being: plentitude, continuity, and graduation. The kingdom of God was gradually and continually advancing in the world, and it would fill the world with all good things. These ideas are the heart of a gospel rooted and grounded in non-biblical thought.

Moral Values

The outworking of the principles of the great chain of being are reflected in Henry May's identification of three central articles of faith that this emerging religion of the nineteenth century embraced.[19] The reality, certainty, and eternity of moral values; a belief in progress; and a belief in culture.

In the broadening of the Christian vison, the narrowness of the biblical morals was one of the first things to go. Morals were understood to be real, certain and eternal but that did not restrict them to being biblically mandated. They were in fact rooted in eternal, autonomous reason. In the Victorian era the lines were starting to be blurred as to what morals were and where they derived from; outward manners were more important than the condition of the heart. Manners were reasonable; something that could not always be said of biblical mandates.

As a result, a problem could be identified and labeled as immoral/sin whether it was biblically wrong or not. Those who had identified the problem would then gather others around them to fight the problem. It was truly a grassroots effort to transform America and it worked wonders. At the same time, there was little

---

18. Marsden, *Understanding Fundamentalism*, 131.
19. May, *End of American Innocence*, 9, 20, 30.

or no government funding for these issues, so the people involved raised the money needed to do whatever it was that they thought needed doing. Large amounts of money were raised and spent on vital issues like education, poverty, horrible living conditions, slavery, child labor, foreign missions, fighting alcohol consumption, voting rights for "all" men, voting rights for women.

America was being transformed by the social gospel of works. The notion of sin had become obsolete; the real battle was against unnatural negative morals that the reformers saw as bad. The gospel was no longer about the condition of the individual before God. It had transformed into the condition of society whose purpose should be meeting the social, economic, and political needs of the people.

This movement was so successful that it continues to influence the way some think about Scripture and Christianity today. For instance, I grew up believing that drinking alcohol was a sin. I was told that the wine that Jesus produced from water in Scripture was not alcoholic; even though the same word was used in the warning to not get drunk. I was blown away one day when in reading the Scriptures I came across a passage in Deut 14:26 speaking in relation to tithing that read: "Bind up the money in your hand and go to the place that the Lord your God chooses and spend the money for whatever you desire—oxen or sheep or wine or strong drink, whatever your appetite craves. And you shall eat there before the Lord your God and rejoice, you and your household." The Bible was telling me that I could go out and buy alcohol, have a party and have fun. I was elated and confused at the same time.

I remember some years later I read that passage in a Bible study and a 90-year-old woman slammed her hand down on the table and said, "That's not in the Bible!" The social gospel of the nineteenth century is still effective in getting its message across to the masses in the twenty-first century.

America was becoming focused on morals while at the same time leaving behind the Bible and its notion of individual sin and the need of salvation. The nineteenth and early twentieth centuries saw the age of the social gospel come into its own and climb to towering heights. Its accomplishments are many: The victory of the North over the South in the war that gave us a new America and an altered constitution, increased voter rights for poor white men, gave women the right to vote, freed blacks, championed public education, instituted prohibition, emphasized manners and cleanliness as opposed to humbleness before God, and opened the door to the eugenics movement to make sure the American race was pure genetically, if not spiritually, just to name a few. All of them were seen as rooted in reality, certain and eternal. These things would always be, of that the reformers had no doubts.

The second belief that the reformers held to be true was a belief in progress. The Puritans had held a strong belief in Postmillennialism, the belief that the kingdom of God would continue to grow until it filled the Earth. That kingdom would last for a thousand years and then Christ would return to start the new age. They believed God had plans for America to be the city on a hill that would usher in the millennial reign. You find those notions throughout the literature of the colonial period.

By the mid-nineteenth century, the millennial kingdom was still being actively sought, especially among the newly emerging middle class. The Industrial Revolution had finally begun to manifest itself on the American continent. The economy was improving rapidly. New signs and wonders were happening all around. The kingdom was surely coming; the only difference between reality and the scriptural version was that this new kingdom was being ushered in by man. It was now the calling of human beings to manifest the kingdom. History (which had been transformed by Hegel into a cheap substitute for God) may play its part in the unfolding of destiny, but humanity must do their part (even if from Hegel's perspective humans were irrelevant because Spirit was all that mattered). The American people must do the actual work of turning their country into the real-world manifestation of the kingdom of God. They must, by sheer force of will, put an end to sin in our midst and advance the new definition of righteousness.

Notice that history became the tool of choice for voicing God's sovereignty, and at the same time God himself was transforming

Fragmentation of Church

his image into an increasingly distant non-personal being that was more Platonic or Deist than biblical. As a result, sin became a problem instead of a condition. The Holy Spirit was renamed hard work. The net result was that the kingdom of God was no longer about God manifesting his power to redeem a people for himself; it was now the responsibility of humanity to manifest the kingdom through their righteous pursuit in their own strength. It was humanity's job to build the kingdom on Earth. Much like the era of the Tower of Babel.

The mainline religion of the nineteenth and early twentieth centuries can be best understood in this context. America was destined to bring the kingdom of God to Earth. The way to do that was not regeneration, it was reform. This was the call that unified Christians, Unitarians, Deists, and just good folks, into what became the driving force of a large portion of America.

Not only was America destined to bring in the kingdom of God to Earth, in the eyes of the reformers, but the kingdom of God would end up looking like America. That brings us to the third area of importance noted by Henry May: a belief in culture. Ever more increasingly the reformers understood Americans to be the custodians of Christian culture. May qualifies this by saying "culture in America meant a particular part of the heritage from the European past, including polite manners, respect for traditional learning, appreciation of the arts, and above all an informed and devoted love of standard literature."[20]

For the social gospel reformers there was little distinction between culture and Christian versus American and Christian. Americans, at least the respectable part of Americans, were the epitome of all those things. In the eyes of the reformers the distinction between America and Christian virtually disappeared. This was possible because of the underlying belief in the great chain of being, especially the notions of plentitude and continuity as specifically applied to America. America is the manifestation of the kingdom of God and therefore the culture of America (which is the kingdom of God by proxy) is destined to fill the Earth.

20. May, *End of American Innocence*, 30.

In our twenty-first century era of aggressive, divisive individuality mixed with a rather tarnished image of what America was, and a lack of any view of the world that is not pragmatic, it is perhaps difficult to understand a large part of a nation joining together in volunteer associations or societies as they were called and in effect transforming a nation in less than a century but that is exactly what happened in America in the nineteenth century.

3

Fragmentation of Science

IN ORDER TO UNDERSTAND the outworking of what was going on in the world of religion it is necessary to have a grasp of the development of "modern" natural science and philosophy because they were the warp and woof of the fabric of society. The following is a brief sketch of the development of what is known as modernity. To begin we will once again examine the work of the British Franciscan monk, William of Ockham.

Nominalism

Ockham, with the exception of his razor, is best known for his use of nominalism defined as: "The doctrine that universals or general ideas are mere names without any corresponding reality. Only particular objects exist, and properties, numbers, and sets are merely features of the way of considering the things that exist."[1] In other words, when I make reference to the man across the street I am speaking of a particular person and therefore a real individual thing. When, however, I speak about "man" in general I am not talking about a real thing but simply a concept that helps

1. "Nominalism," *English Oxford Living Dictionary*.

me understand things that actually exist. This word "man" that I use universally is nothing more than a sign which stands for many things. In doing so, Ockham made a radical shift away from the established Aristotelian-Thomistic view of knowledge which was grounded in divine "reason" or from another perspective, in eternal forms in the mind of God which were essentially the blueprints of the material world. Such ideas are totally rooted in Greek philosophy.

Ockham rejected this notion of eternal forms in the mind of God because to him it was antithetical to God's sovereign nature. Forms stood in the way of God's freedom. So, to give God his freedom, Ockham gave God the gift of despotism coupled with arbitrariness and invested him with absolute, free power. The only thing that Ockham's God could not do was contradict himself.

In such a world, God "can, if he wishes, make it meritorious for us to hate Him. Hatred of God, theft, and adultery are all bad only because of the will of God, not for any intelligible reason. So, too, God can make fire cool, just as easily as he makes it heat, for there is no necessary connection between cause and effect."[2] Therefore, humans must submit to the law of God simply because God has made these laws and not others. There is no reason except for the reason that this is what the sovereign has proclaimed. In becoming an arbitrary despot with absolute, free power, God lost his character. His laws no longer flowed out of his righteousness, justice, and mercy. They simply flowed from whim.

In this regard, Dooyeweerd notes: ". . .that Ockham deprived the law of its intrinsic value. Founded in an incalculable, arbitrary God who is bound to nothing, the law only held for the sinful realm of nature. For Ockham, one is never certain that God's will would not change under different circumstances."[3]

This was a radical, new understanding of the way the world operated. In fact, it was so radical that it began to put a stake in the heart of the Middle Ages. It was noted in the previous chapter there were only two options, the first was the Reformation which

---

2. Maurer, "Scotism and Ockhamism," 222.
3. Dooyeweerd, *Roots of Western Culture*, 138.

Fragmentation of Science

was examined in the chapter on religion. The second path, which is the subject of the present chapter was more "in line with the new motive of nature severed from the faith of the church, [it] establish a modern view of life concentrated on the religion of human personality" and led to the development of modern humanism.[4]

It should be noted that the death of the scholastic Aristotelian-Thomistic view of the world was not quick and easy. In fact, to paraphrase words often attributed to Mark Twain, the report of its death has been grossly exaggerated. Scholasticism never completely died. It may have been in recovery for some time but eventually it raised its head in both Protestant and reformed Catholic versions which are still with us today.[5] The remainder of this chapter will focus on the development of the new scientific way of thinking that emerged during the Renaissance and the changes in philosophy that accompanied that new view of the world until the seeds of fragmentation, which it planted, began to grow.

In spite of Ockham's breakthrough with nominalism in the fourteenth century, in the next hundred years, most of what occurred in philosophical and theological circles was simply a wrangling over words—philology dominated the period. At the same time, however, there was a revival in the interest in Plato and Neoplatonism and along with it came a resurgence of artistic activity. It seemed as if there was a spiritual revival beginning to take place in nearly every area of life except philosophy.[6]

The old dialectic of nature-grace was beginning to disintegrate and a new, seemingly spiritual, revival was coming from a new foundation of understanding, that of human freedom. "This new dialectic motive rests on an absolute secularization of the biblical nature of creation and Christian freedom (as a fruit of redemption)."[7] The radicalness of this new freedom cannot be overemphasized. Out of the nominalism of Ockham, a new understanding of the individual as absolutely autonomous was

---

4. Dooyeweerd, *Roots*, 139.
5. VanderStelt, *Philosophy and Scripture*, 268–90.
6. Cassierer, *Individual and the Cosmos*, 1–6.
7. Dooyeweerd, *New Critique of Theoretical Thought*, vol. 1, 190.

beginning to develop. Dooyeweerd writes: "this implies a rejection of all faith in authority and of any conception according to which man is subjected to a law not imposed by his own reason."[8]

Slowly, the individualism that Ockham had applied to all things began to become the main thrust of human existence. The individual had somehow managed to claw its way out of the mass of humanity dominated by environment, and circumstance. The result was that humanity deemed it possible to break free from its Creator, and simply declare "*I am*." I am the master of my own destiny. I can choose to believe what I want to believe. I can choose to believe in God or not. For the first time in the history of the world human personality guided by autonomous reason stood face to face with nature and strove to dominate it. Of course, these kinds of thought were only on the minds of those with enough economic stability to not worry about their next meal—they were strongly aristocratic in origin.[9]

It is here, in the struggle of the newly freed aristocratic personality standing against "immeasurable nature," that the new dialectic of nature-freedom began to unfold. The creation of that new understanding of nature began to develop more fully through the work of Nicholas Cusanus (1401–64). Cusanus moves forward by turning to the past and resurrecting Plato to deliver the world from Aristotle. Yet, this resurrection is more like a transformation, for Cusanus takes the foundation of Plato's mathematical understanding of the world and turns it on its head.

For Plato, the purpose of the true philosopher is preliminary instruction and not strictly empirical. His goal is not to understand the sensual world in its own right but to uncover its soul which is to be found outside temporal reality in the eternal world of Ideas, the real forms of all that exists in the sensual world, through the power of mathematics. It must be noted that transforming Plato's forms into mathematical formulas was a giant leap of faith.

Cusanus rejects both Plato's notion of eternal forms outside the sensual world and Aristotle's notion of the ideas (his word for

---

8. Dooyeweerd, *New Critique of Theoretical Thought*, vol. 1, 191.
9. Dooyeweerd, *New Critique of Theoretical Thought*, vol. 1, 192.

Fragmentation of Science

eternal forms) residing in the mind of God. Reality is no longer to be found in the eternal realm of perfect forms but in the empirical realm of experience. Cusanus understood these things but only from a distance. He had a *viso intellectus*, an intellectual vision. He could see the goal, but he could not find the path to get there in his own time. It would remain for others to blaze the trail of faith in mathematics.

The first to begin to explore Cusanus's new path of faith was the artist Leonardo da Vinci (1452–1519) He continued the mathematical study of nature started by Cusanus. This new way of study required eyes that were capable of seeing nature as a system, a whole and complete system thoroughly ordered in every way. This wholeness was to be understood, not in some mystical way, but in a logical way that was consistent with its orderliness. Only mathematics could accomplish this goal.

Leonardo was continually railing against the supposed scholars who did not have the faith to see the certainty of mathematical equations and often resorted to mysticism to explain the workings of nature. He wrote in one of his notebooks: "Oh! human stupidity, do you not perceive that, though you have been with yourself all your life, you are not yet aware of the thing you possess most of, that is of your folly? And then, with the crowd of sophists, you deceive yourselves and others, despising the mathematical sciences, in which truth dwells and the knowledge of the things included in them."[10]

Science for him was devoted to understanding the workings of the natural world. And mathematics was the key to understanding those works. For Leonardo the forms of nature are all around us, not in a distant eternal realm. His own words speak volumes on this matter: "There is no certainty in sciences where one of the mathematical sciences cannot be applied, or which are not in relation with these mathematics."[11]

A true Renaissance man, Leonardo da Vinci developed the new understanding of mathematics in a diverse variety of areas

10. da Vinci, *Notebooks*, loc. 1210.
11. da Vinci, *Notebooks*, loc. 1158.

including, art, anatomy, botany, geography, physical science, astronomy, mechanics, architecture, inventions and experiments.[12] In doing so he helped to advance Cusanus's intellectual vision of the material world interpreted via mathematics.

However, even though he "anticipated Galileo's mathematical-mechanical analysis of empirical phenomena, he continued to conceive of nature as a teleological whole animated with life."[13] Much like Cusanus, he could see the world to come but he could not fathom taking the leap of faith it would take to get there.

All of that would change with the birth of modern natural science which came into being through the work of Kepler (1551–1630), Galileo (1564–1642) and Newton (1642–1726). These men began the work of moving away from the scholastic notion of "substance" which was rooted in Aristotle's notion of reality. "The philosophical term 'substance' corresponds to the Greek *ousia*, which means 'being', transmitted via the Latin *substantia*, which means 'something that stands under or grounds things.' According to the generic sense, therefore, the substances in a given philosophical system are those things which, according to that system, are the foundational or fundamental entities of reality."[14]

Mathematics and Theoretical Thought

In other words, substance describes individual things in themselves, entities apart from their properties. When Leonardo used mathematics to explain reality, he was dealing with the things in themselves, physical elements of the world. Kepler, Galileo and Newton abandoned that method with a huge leap of faith. Instead of starting with the things themselves, these men started with mathematics: "in order to scientifically investigate the physical aspect of reality by means of analytical and synthetical mathematical thought. With its concept of function, modern science wished to

---

12. Vinci, *The Notebooks XIX*.
13. Dooyeweerd, *New Critique of Theoretical Thought*, vol. 1, 198.
14. "Substance," *Stanford Encyclopedia of Philosophy*.

grasp the functional coherence of physical phenomena in mathematically formulated natural laws . . . Galileo's postulate for the modern physical method implied a reduction of all qualitative distinctions . . . to mathematically determined differences of motion. According to its science-ideal, Humanistic philosophy now sought to apply this postulate to all other aspects of reality in order to construe a continuous mechanical image of the world."[15]

Theoretical thought is just that—theoretical. It does not start with material reality. These mathematicians do not begin with a *Ding an sich* (a thing in itself) and discover the mathematical properties of that specific thing. On the contrary, they begin with a theoretical hypothesis that may or may not have a correlation with reality and continue to tweak both the hypothesis and the mathematics until the math actually works consistently. Being applicable to the actual world of time and space as it exists is irrelevant as long as the mathematics works.

Mathematical truths are more real than the sensual world in which we live. In the new science, mathematical theorems are the "substance" of reality. This shift toward theoretical thought did not happen overnight. It took centuries to develop. The creation of analytical geometry by Descartes and analytical calculus by Leibniz would have to be realized before this shift could come to fruition. In the meantime, the mathematical journey from Galileo to Leibniz had to pass through the mind of Pierre Gassendi (1592–1631).

Pierre Gassendi

Pierre Gassendi, a colleague of Galileo's, sought to remove himself from the forms of Aristotle and Plato and as a result embraced the ideas of the Atomists. There was, however, a problem with doing so. The philosophy of Democratus, Leucippos, Epicurus and Lucretius evoked a tendency within the church to think of atheism. In seventeenth century Europe, that was a charge to be avoided if one valued one's life. The reason for this proclivity to be seen as

---

15. Dooyeweerd, *New Critique of Theoretical Thought*, vol. 1, 201.

atheistic was threefold: indivisibility, materialism, and determinism.[16] First, if everything is simply matter, how does one explain both movement and individuation? Second, Epicurus, and for that matter almost all Greek thought, began with the concept that "nothing comes into being out of what is not" which is completely antithetical to the biblical notion of creation ex nihilo.[17]

The corollary to the atomist's understanding of matter is that it never really goes away; it simply changes form. This infers that matter is therefore eternal. This especially lent suspicion to the charge of being atheistic. And thirdly, with regard to determinism: If all is nothing but matter in motion there can be no room for anything except cause and effect. Everything happens because of something else stretching back all the way to the first swerve of an atom into another atom.

Gassendi "Christianized" the notions of the atomists by introducing "two traditional Christian doctrines, providence and free will, into his revamped version of Epicureanism."[18] As noted earlier, in standard Epicureanism, if the world is nothing but material atoms then the only way for there to be movement in the world, as we know it, is through collisions. At some point in some time one atom swerved into another and became the first cause of movement. Chance reigned supreme.

In order to circumvent this problem Gassendi simply attributed all movement to the providence of God. He writes: "It may be supposed that the individual atoms received from God as he created them their corpulence, or dimensions, however small, and their shapes in ineffable variety, and likewise they received the capacity [vis] requisite to moving, to imparting motion to others. . .all this to the degree that he foresaw would be necessary for every purpose and effect that he destined them for."[19] God is now reduced to being nothing more than the God of the swerve.

---

16. Gaukroger, *Emergence of Scientific Culture*, 157–322.
17. Gaukroger, *Emergence of Scientific Culture*, 265.
18. Gaukroger, *Emergence of Scientific Culture*, 274.
19. Gassendi, *Selected Works of Pierre Gassendi*, 280.

Fragmentation of Science

This shift in direction is much more than a rehashing of Aristotelian intrinsic natural goal-directedness of specific types in nature such as an acorn turning into an oak tree. For Gassendi, individual atoms have no purpose or no direction in and of themselves. They were simply moved upon by the original stirring of the hand of God. God was present at the beginning and the outcome of his stirring is all that we see and all that we see is the outworking of motion set into play by the hand of God. The difference between Gassendi's atomistic world and the Epicurean's is that the former "has the distinct advantage that it accounts for the organized complexity that we find in the natural world, whereas it is a mystery how this comes about on the Epicurean picture."[20]

The problem with providence in a mechanistic understanding of the world is that it leaves no place for individual freedom. Man becomes nothing more than another brick in the wall where he is welcomed into the machine called the universe. Meaning is destroyed. Gassendi tried to restore meaning and freedom by resorting to material-mind dualism. The intellect has its own nature that is separate (somehow) from the outworking of the material world.

In the end Gassendi's christianized Epicurean view of the world dominated natural philosophy and science for nearly three hundred years. On a secondary level, it also became the dominant way that the concept of the sovereignty of God was understood in Protestant circles. It transformed theology as well as philosophy.

While Gassendi found a way to make a materialist understanding of the world theologically acceptable, three others, Kepler, Galileo, and Newton, though rooted and grounded in a theological understanding of God's world in keeping "with the intensely pious character of the century," [ended up] "doing something very radical that would eventually tear Western civilization from its religious mooring" and its mooring in created reality.[21] They began to take the material world out of materialism.

---

20. Gaukroger, *Emergence of Scientific Culture*, 275.
21. Barrett, *Death of the Soul*, 4.

New Science

While heavily dependent upon the ideas of the past, especially the Greeks, the makers of the new science managed to transform the meaning of the words of the past into a theoretical mathematical understanding of nature that they called "the new science."[22] The depth of that newness would not be understood for over a century but in the short term what they were constructing was the notion of nature as a mathematical machine.

However, if nature was becoming a machine, what was to become of the individual? The new science began to develop the nature aspect of dialectical struggle between personal freedom and the determinism of "nature the machine." With regard to this new struggle, William Barrett writes: "The presence of mind is everywhere in the formulation of this [New] science, and yet the results of this science were to be alleged as evidence for some general mechanistic view of the world, according to which the human mind appears as feeble and unfree. That is a paradox and an irony that ever since have haunted the thinking of our modern epoch...Yet with all its inherent paradoxes, scientific materialism was to become de facto the dominant mentality of the West in the three and a half centuries that followed."[23]

The interesting thing about its reign over science is that it was and still is covert, not overt. It is the unspoken presupposition that still dominates the habits, attitudes, and prejudices of the practitioners of science today.[24]

Math and the Real World . . . Again

Certainly, these men talked about the *Ding an sich* or the thing in itself and they still believed in the existence of the real world but they were laying a foundation from which there could be no contact with the thing in itself. Dooyeweerd writes:

22. Barrett, *Death of the Soul*, 4.
23. Barrett, *Death of the Soul*, 6–7.
24. Barrett, *Death of the Soul*, 6–7.

"We may not close our eyes to the new peculiar sense which the concept of substance [the thing in itself] acquires in humanistic philosophy. It is the basic structure of humanistic transcendental ground-idea which is responsible for this new meaning. In this humanistic philosophy the criterion of truth is not sought in agreement between thought and 'the essences of reality outside our mind' [the things themselves]. It is sought in thought itself with the geometrically attained clearness and distinction of concepts."[25]

With the work of Leibniz analytic calculus would create even clearer and more distinct concepts. This was the seed of fragmentation. It was there in these men's work; but they could not or would not see it. Instead, they continued to work through the external ramifications of their work on the newly reformed concept of Mechanism. The problem at hand seemed to be that it created a split between the material world and this "thing" called mind. Gassendi was certainly aware of the problem and so too was the natural philosopher Rene Descartes, a contemporary and competitor of Gassendi's. Though in modern times Descartes is most famous for his philosophy of doubt and the statement "I think therefore I am," and equally infamous on many modern high school campuses for developing analytical geometry, he was as much an advocate of Mechanism as Gassendi. In fact, his adaptation of Mechanism dominated until the Mechanist work of Isaac Newton in the early seventeenth century.

Descartes (1596–1650)

In summarizing the work of Descartes, Albert Ramsperger writes: "given a certain arrangement of matter expressible in mathematical terms, and the laws of motion, we have all that is necessary to make a world and to determine by mathematical calculations all that will happen there. Even living things, insofar as they are bodies without minds or souls, are mere mechanical automata and

---

25. Dooyeweerd, *New Critique of Theoretical Thought*, vol. 1, 203.

Descartes believed that all earthly creatures except man are but complicated machines."[26]

How is humanity to escape being a machine? Descartes takes the work of re-describing physical phenomena in a way that is amenable to mechanist theory begun by Gassendi and Thomas Hobbes (1588–1679) and synthesizes it with the work of Isaac Beekman (1588–1637) and his notions of the process of Mechanism. The result is the most comprehensive understanding of Mechanism during the 1630s and 1640s. It would only be surpassed by the work of Isaac Newton in 1687.[27]

Gaukroger notes that Descartes began his work by "establishing natural philosophy as a legitimate exercise [which] requires us to separate the physical world from mind, in that the physical world cannot harbor the intentions, goals, and aims that we treat as characteristic of mind, and from God, in that God is not immanent in his creation but transcends it."[28]

This dualism was seen to be necessary if human freedom was to continue to exist. Therefore, Descartes had to begin not with matter but with the self, "I think, therefore I am." In doing so "he made the 'rational soul' independent as a 'thinking substance' in opposition to the 'corporeal world.'"[29] This dualism of mind and body was the only hope for the freedom of mathematical thought, as well as the freedom of humanity from becoming just another cog in the machine of the universe.

Isaac Newton

The goal of mathematical natural philosophy was the underlying presupposition behind the pursuit of the mechanist projects of the seventeenth eighteenth century. The process of moving beyond the material order to explain the material order was elusive to say

26. Ramsperger, *History of Philosophical Systems*, 243.
27. Gaukroger, *Emergence*, 289.
28. Gaukroger, *Emergence*, 290.
29. Dooyeweerd, *Reformation and Scholasticism in Philosophy*, vol. 2, 182.

Fragmentation of Science

the least.[30] Isaac Newton helped solidify the move toward a purely mathematical explanation of the material world by breaking away from both Aristotelian and Cartesian theories. He began to provide a comprehensive account of various aspects of the material world by going "beyond practical mathematics and turning it into a part of natural philosophy."[31]

In doing so his thinking produced a paradigm shift of monumental proportions. Newton was no longer concerned with theories of matter but now solely focused on theories of mathematics. It is this shift in thinking that completely separates the new science from the material world. It is, in the words of Herman Dooyeweerd: "The development of a new metaphysic. It was supposed that the true essences, the super-temporal substance of 'reality in itself' could only be grasped by the new mathematical method of thought."[32] With this new concept of substance, "as it was defined by Leibniz, the modern functional concept of law came into being. The functional coherence between variant phenomena, construed by thought, becomes the "invariant", the substance of reality."[33] In other words mathematical theories became the glue that holds reality together.

Gottfried Wilhelm Leibniz (1646–1716)

Leibniz would have nothing to do with a world ruled by inertia. His world would be ruled by energy. Certainly, he did not deny that matter existed, but it was not the unifying aspect of the universe. For example, if one were to look at a table sitting in the middle of the room with materialist eyes, one would see individual atoms somehow attracted to one another, but the oneness of the table might be hard to explain.

30. Gaukroger, *Emergence*, 400.
31. Gaukroger, *Emergence* 395.
32. Dooyeweerd, *New Critique of Theoretical Thought*, vol. 1, 201–2.
33. Dooyeweerd, *New Critique of Theoretical Thought*, vol. 1, 202.

Louder Than Words

Leibniz, on the other hand, understood the table as one, in other words, a whole. Yes, it is made up of molecules of matter but there is something else that unifies all those various pieces and makes them one. For Leibniz the unifying factor is energy and this "energy" he called monads.

This is a radical step away from a strict materialistic mechanistic view of the world because no longer is the world controlled by secondhand energy produced through inertia. For Leibniz, energy becomes self-generating. The end result is that the mind, seen to be passive in Mechanism and in later British Empiricism, is now active; it pursues knowledge (Continental school of philosophy) instead of receiving it (British school of philosophy).

Leibniz sees this energy and the monads which produce it as an outgrowth of spirit. Mathematical thought then, is a spiritual experience. These energetic monads are not just waiting for something to happen to them. They are, in one sense, generating their own destiny. Smaller monads make up larger monads, and those larger monads form together and create the "I" that is me. I am a monad made up of monads. I am composed of self-generating energy. I am not simply a composition of mindless molecules. For Leibniz, this energy is the essence of our freedom as human beings.

Monads completely fill the space of the cosmos. For Leibniz individual monads are a living representation of the universe, yet they are completely self-sufficient. "In this way the noumenal metaphysical cosmos was resolved into an infinite multitude of 'windowless' monads; spaceless, animated points of force."[34] These points have no real existence in our "world as it appears in space.'" But in the world of metaphysics, accessible only to theoretic thinking, a point has, Leibniz said, a deeper reality.[35] In all of this, mathematical thought has taken the place of the material world. Science interprets the "real world" through mathematical equations.

The "new science" has removed humanity from reality. The question ceases to be: How shall we then live? And becomes: Is reality real? Yet, the world kept on turning, people kept on living, life

---

34. Dooyeweerd, *New Critique of Theoretical Thought*, vol. 1, 230.
35. Dooyeweerd, *Reformation and Scholasticism in Philosophy*, vol. 2, 184.

unfolded as it always had. The problem was there was no longer a foundation for hope in those who understood what was going on. Certainly, the increasing ephemeral status of humanity since the eighteenth century has caused many to say: "Something's happening all around us, but we cannot quite put our finger on it." We still do not have a clue.

4

Fragmentation of Work

THE AMERICAN INDUSTRIAL REVOLUTION which occurred primarily in the nineteenth and early twentieth century is nothing short of a miracle. Whether one believes it was "manifest destiny," the advance of the scientific point of view, or a mixture of both, all can agree that something took place in just over one hundred years that had never happened before in the history of the world. What follows is a brief synopsis of what might be called the second American Revolution.

At the time of the original American Revolution, the country was a farming nation. "It is estimated that in America's formative years, nine out of ten Americans made their livelihood through agriculture."[1] Thomas Jefferson saw the stability of the new nation rooted in that agrarian lifestyle, writing: "The small landholders are the most precious part of the State. . .those who labor in the earth are the chosen people of God, if ever He had a chosen people, whose breasts he had made his peculiar deposit."[2]

---

1. Hillstrom and Hillstrom, *Industrial Revolution in America*, vol. 8, 1.
2. Hillstrom and Hillstrom, *Industrial Revolution in America*, vol. 8, 1.

Fragmentation of Work

The Second American Revolution

It is hard to pinpoint what exactly started the Industrial Revolution. Certainly, the mass production of pottery and textiles in England were the beginnings of manufacturing on a large scale. However, both of those endeavors were dependent upon the revolution in the production of iron which was dependent upon the inventions of new machines and processes that allowed a better quality of iron to be made by burning coal (which was plentiful) instead of charcoal (trees were getting scarce in England). For without improved iron, the materials with which to build the steam engine would not have been of a sufficient quality to work efficiently over the long haul. It was the steam engine that would power the new machines that were used to make both pottery and textiles. These prerequisites for the emergence of the Industrial Revolution began to be developed in the mid-eighteenth century.

When the English began mass-producing textiles in the early nineteenth century the demand for cotton became intense. However, "English manufacturers had set little value on the 13 colonies as a source on which to draw for raw cotton," because the short-staple type cotton Americans produced was too expensive to produce due to the difficulty of removing the seeds.[3]

It is here that America made its first move toward the Industrial Revolution: Eli Whitney invented a machine called the cotton gin which removed the seeds from the short-staple cotton mechanically, allowing American cotton to be priced competitively in the world market. The result was that "the United States rapidly became the most important source in the world" for cotton.[4] America's Industrial Revolution began with an agricultural revolution.

As a result, the textile industry began to explode in America. "In 1800 America had two cotton mills; in 1810, one hundred and two" mills, thanks to two Americans who were able to memorize the workings of modern textile mills they had visited in England

---

3. Hammond, *Religion and Personal Autonomy*, 183–84.
4. Hammond, *Religion and Personal Autonomy*, 183–84.

and then reproduce them at home.⁵ It was the American cotton boom in the South and the resulting mass production of textiles in the North that opened the door for further industrial expansion in America.

Transportation

Cotton and the resulting textile goods had to be transported to their destinations and transportation was expensive; initially averaging a hundred dollars a ton. The government and private sector worked together and began constructing canals to improve access to markets in the newly acquired Northwest (which at the time consisted of Wisconsin, Illinois, Michigan, and Ohio). The Erie Canal was completed in 1825. "This engineering marvel gave farmers in Michigan, Illinois, Ohio, and Wisconsin the inexpensive transportation artery they needed to send their products to the big cities of the East."⁶ As a result the cost of shipping per ton decreased to fifteen dollars a ton which led to a great increase in the trafficking of goods both to and from the big cities.

With new transportation avenues available it was not long before transportation itself began to improve. The newly developed steam engine began to be fitted to power ships in the 1780s. It was not until "August 18, 1807, [that Robert] Fulton launched what is now regarded as the first practical, operational steamboat into U.S. waters. His boat, called the North River Steamboat (not the Clermont, as erroneously reported in countless textbooks over the years), set out from New York City and made its way 150 miles upstream to Albany."⁷

Steam shipping revolutionized both the transportation of goods and people in America. The problem was that it was limited by access to navigable waterways. A steam engine that could travel across land would improve the transportation system even more.

5. Hammond, *Religion and Personal Autonomy*, 183–84.
6. Hillstrom and Hillstrom, *Industrial Revolution in America*, vol. 9, 16.
7. Hillstrom and Hillstrom, *Industrial Revolution in America*, vol. 3, 5.

Fragmentation of Work

In 1815 the first charter for a railroad was issued but never left the drawing board. It was not until thirteen years later that a group of businessmen in Baltimore began earnest planning and construction of a railroad line whose name is etched into the hearts of all who have ever played the game *Monopoly*: the B&O. Two years later the train was able to travel on thirteen miles of track.

"Building the railroad became Baltimore's greatest civic project. It was considered a national endeavor at the time, and its history is to a large extent the history of all early railroads."[8] By the 1840s railroads were spreading across the eastern United States and winding their way through the Appalachian Mountains into the Midwest at a tremendous pace.

In one sense, the spread of the railroad westward reflected the notion of "manifest destiny" that filled the hearts of most people in America. The move west was facilitated by government expansion with the Louisiana Purchase, the Northwest Purchase and the Mexican American war that gave us Texas, the Southwest and California.

The call was to advance the millennial kingdom by filling America from coast to coast with the fruit of her efforts. Interestingly enough, the concept of filling the nation was rooted in the platonic notion of the great chain of being. Railroads were the fastest and most efficient way to do that. "By 1860 Chicago was being served by eleven different railroads, including the mighty Illinois Central, and it had become the undisputed railroad center of the nation."[9]

Simultaneous

It is important to remember that none of these new developments were happening in isolation. Everything was changing everywhere. Steam power changed transportation; transportation expanded where people could live and what goods could be delivered there.

---

8. Diltz, *Great Road*, 2.
9. Hillstrom and Hillstrom, *Industrial Revolution in America*, vol. 2, 13.

The advance toward the West was enabled by the increase in population from immigration that was facilitated by steam powered ocean vessels that made crossing the Atlantic quicker and cheaper. The use of steam power facilitated an increase in coal production. All these things needed laborers to build, maintain, and use. Such changes opened the door to employment opportunities away from the farm.

Urbanization meant that there were fewer people in rural areas while at the same time, with the nation increasing in population and physical size, there was more demand than ever for the products of agriculture and meat packing. Chicago became the railroad center of the nation because it had become the meat packing center of the nation. From the West and Midwest came the cattle by train. Out of the loading docks in every direction came the processed meat of the packing houses in newly developed refrigerated box cars to feed the growing population. Steam power was also harnessed to tractors, harvesters, and other machinery, so fewer laborers were needed to produce more food.

The prophesied "manifest destiny" was bringing forth new and wonderful things across the expanding nation in what, at the time, probably seemed like lightning speed. Part of that speed was to be found in the development of electricity for human use. Benjamin Franklin had caught it with his kite and key. From there he developed the use of the lightning rod and other ideas about electricity in the late eighteenth century. Others took his ideas, combined them with the study of magnetism, and by 1831 had created the first electric motor.

By 1838 Samuel Morse had developed a communication system that could pass through a single electric wire. The owners of the railroads quickly saw the use of such an immediate mode of communication and as they laid tracks for their trains around the continent, they also ran electrical lines to communicate in real time with Morse code across vast stretches of land. By 1861 there were Western Union offices at every train stop and telegraph poles and lines were a part of the national landscape. Fifteen years later Morse's code would begin to be broken by Alexander Graham

Fragmentation of Work

Bell's telephone. At nearly the same time, in 1879, Thomas Edison found a way to create light using the same electrical wire.

All these amazing innovations were working their way into the limelight while the development of new high quality steel was being ironed out. As Hoerr notes "Iron had served its purpose in the early stages of the Industrial Revolution, but the infrastructure for the next great leap—railroads, bridges, factories, and office buildings—required a stronger, less malleable material."[10] With this new and improved steel, cities began to move up as well as out and the skyscraper was born.

Not only did men begin to make steel but steel also began to make men—into millionaires. Andrew Carnegie and J.P. Morgan turned steel into gold while the alchemy of Cornelius Vanderbilt and J.D. Rockefeller did the same with transportation and oil. As a result, they became men of power and influence—the robber barons, as they were known by some, who turned business on its ear, creating the corporation, conglomerations, and monopolies. In the process they opened the door to a new level of strife between labor and management, thus facilitating the rise of unions.

In the early days of the oil business gasoline was a waste product that was burned off so that kerosene could be produced. Kerosene was the fuel in demand for lamps throughout the nineteenth century.[11] In 1872–3, "American engineer George Brayton developed a two-stroke kerosene engine. It is considered to be the first safe and practical oil engine."[12]

With the development of the automobile in the late nineteenth century gasoline became the in-demand fuel for transportation. Coincidentally, "new oil discoveries in Texas brought the price of oil and gasoline to record lows.[13] The demand for this new mode of transportation began to increase and a new way of manufacturing

10. Hoerr, *Wolf Finally Came*, 84.
11. "Petroleum Technology History," Great Achievements, https://www.greatachievements.org/?id=3677.
12. "Internal Combustion Engine," Live Science, https://www.livescience.com/37538-who-invented-the-car.html.
13. Hillstrom and Hillstrom, *Industrial Revolution in America*, vol. 9, 55.

was developed. It was called the assembly line. The car that was produced there was the Ford Model T. Henry Ford was able to produce this easy to drive and relatively inexpensive automobile by using the division of labor and interchangeable parts. The automobiles moved through the factory on conveyor belts and were assembled by men in stationary places next to the moving parts. It was another revolution in the manufacturing process.[14] Following in Ford's footsteps marketing companies in the 1950s would encourage Americans to "Drive the USA in your Chevrolet" as new model cars would roll off the assembly line every year.

Good Times, Bad Times

One could perhaps best describe the so-called age of manifest destiny and Industrial Revolution in the words of Charles Dickens:

> It was the best of times, it was the worst of times, it was the age of wisdom, it was the age of foolishness, it was the epoch of belief, it was the epoch of incredulity, it was the season of light, it was the season of darkness, it was the spring of hope, it was the winter of despair.[15]

One thing is for sure: no stone was left unturned, and no one was left untouched. The revolution transformed America. For example, in 1840, 69 percent of the population was still engaged in farm-related work for their sustenance.[16] But by the 1890s manufacturing output surpassed agricultural output.[17] By the beginning of the twentieth century the value of manufacturing was more than double that of agriculture. At the end of the first decade of the twentieth century America was far beyond the rest of the world as leader in manufacturing.[18]

---

14. Hillstrom and Hillstrom, *Industrial Revolution in America*, vol. 9, 56.
15. Dickens, *Tale of Two Cities*, 39.
16. Hillstrom and Hillstrom, *Industrial Revolution in America*, vol. 9, 3.
17. Hillstrom and Hillstrom, *Industrial Revolution in America*, vol. 9, 9.
18. Hillstrom and Hillstrom, *Industrial Revolution in America*, vol. 9, 19–20.

Fragmentation of Work

Farming did maintain its position as the single largest industry. Land prices were increasing, the amount of food being produced was increasing through innovation and invention, but the number of people living and working on farms was being drastically reduced. People were moving to the cities for work because to most it seemed that was where the new money economy was flowing from.

Population statistics show this to be true. "In 1800 less than four percent of America's population was living in centers of population greater than 10,000." By 1850 it rose to 12 percent and by 1880 75 percent of the American population lived in urban cities.[19] The new industrial economy created a demand for jobs that was heretofore unheard of. However, the rural population moving into the cities could not begin to fill the need for workers, so immigration came to the rescue, resulting in over twenty-seven million immigrants entering the United States between 1819 and 1910. Approximately 64 percent of those immigrants arrived between the years of 1881 and 1910.[20]

New York (a prime example of an established city) and Chicago (representing the new frontier) will suffice as examples of rapid urban growth. In 1880 the population of New York was 1,206,299. By 1910 it had grown to 4,766,883, an increase of nearly 400 percent.[21] Out on the frontier in 1880 Chicago, which was just recovering from the great fire of 1871, had a population of 503,185. By 1910 it had grown by over 400 percent to 2,185,283 and had taken on the moniker of the Second City.[22]

---

19. Hillstrom and Hillstrom, *Industrial Revolution in America*, vol. 9, 201.

20. Dunlevy, *Economic Opportunity*, 75–92.

21. New York City Government, "New York City Planning," https://www1.nyc.gov/assets/planning/download/pdf/planning-level/nyc-population/historical-population/1790-2000_nyc_foreign_birth_graph.pdf.

22. Weintraub, "Why They Call It the Second City," https://chicagoreader.com/news-politics/why-they-call-it-the-second-city/.

Louder Than Words

Breakdown of the Family

Such rapid growth might have been good for industry but for individuals and families it was nothing short of a tsunami of change that completely wiped out the way life had existed for centuries. In preindustrial America, families were the center of the economy. Those families were largely rooted in agricultural endeavors. The entire family worked together—father, mother and children doing what needed to be done in order that the family could, literally, survive. The hope was that if they were diligent, they would eventually prosper—at least in theory. Theory, however, may not have been close to reality in many cases; for the above population figures note when the opportunity came to leave the farm, people did so in droves.

Farming was a hard life. But the agricultural family unit was relatively cohesive. It had to be if they were to survive. The transition to urban life or industrial life broke that cohesion. Once in the city, the family, even the children (as young as four or five years old), began to work in various industries. They might have all worked at the same factory but more than likely they were working in jobs segregated by gender and age, as well as location. Labor was being divided and time became a premium. Like life on the farm, the days were long, twelve to fourteen hours a day, but unlike the farm those days were spent doing a single task repeatedly with no family interaction and a task master making sure production quotas were being met.

When they returned home after work, it was more than likely not a home that they were used to, nor was it "their" home. They were tenants living in tenements. With the rapid increase in population came the rapid construction of shelters, more often than not, built with less than quality construction mixed with inadequate plumbing, poor heating and little privacy. In some areas of Manhattan around 1910 the population density was over five hundred persons per acre.[23] To get an idea of just how closely packed those

---

23. New York City Government, "New York City Planning," https://www1.nyc.gov/assets/planning/download/pdf/data-maps/nyc-population/

Fragmentation of Work

people were back then consider that "the most densely populated modern capital city in the world, the City of Manila, where over 1.6 million people are packed into some 38.55 square kilometers of land area, or 9,526 acres, has a population density of roughly 173 persons per acre."[24] Manhattan today averages 105 persons per acre.[25]

For most, it was a shock to the system. The workday was becoming increasingly structured in a rigid way that had never existed before. Free time, what little there was of it, consisted mostly of exhaustion, making something to eat and going to bed. The body was worked to a frazzle, but the mind was being numbed to near senselessness by mindless repetitive tasks required in the factory. The new factory labor jobs were mostly being filled with dark white immigrants from Eastern and Southern Europe who were largely unskilled, non-English speaking and illiterate.

It was in this cavern of urban industrial milieu when the rich were very rich, and the poor were very poor, that the need for a new kind of man began to emerge. It was the need for someone to keep production flowing smoothly. Out of the fray of the dispensable common workers rose individuals who were not owners and who were not workers; they were managers. This new breed of man began to make more money than the workers and yet less than the owners. They were stuck in the middle with clowns to the left of them and jokers to the right; a distinct middle class began to come into its own.

In less than one hundred years an entire country was turned upside down. More than that, it was fragmented in ways that no one had ever experienced before. Life as it had been known ceased to exist for the majority of Americans.

---

historical-population/1910_pop_density.pdf.

24. https://worldpopulationreview.com/world-cities/manila-population.

25. New York City Government, "New York City Planning," https://www1.nyc.gov/assets/planning/download/pdf/data-maps/nyc-population/census2010/t_pl_p5_nyc.pdf

5

Fragmentation of Philosophy

THE NEW SCIENCE COMPLETED the transition of the world from a creation in which the human race could flourish into a great machine, perhaps a huge clock that pressed ahead regardless of what the various parts did. It is important to understand that every day, ordinary people did not know that the creation had changed, because it really had not. But the movers and shakers understood that something was going on even if the plebs were clueless.

Hume, Kant, and Hegel tried their best to bring a bit of humanity back to the human race but, because they could not or would not think biblically about the nature of the world, the best they could do was find a way for a ghost to enter the machine. Hume and Kant, from the position of science at the time, understood that humans could not directly interact with the machine.

Hume understood that all we have are sense impressions and that we cannot know for certain whether the objects of those impressions exist in and of themselves or not. Kant was clear that humans never encounter the *Ding and sich*, the thing-in-itself (which includes the entire world). It is important to understand that given their presuppositions about reality they are 100 percent correct. That is not the same as saying their presuppositions are correct.

Fragmentation of Philosophy

Hegel wanted to move away from the potential skepticism of both Hume and Kant, so he planted the roots of his philosophy in *Geist*, the German word for spirit or mind. From his perspective this Spirit is Absolute for it produces itself and all that is within itself, in a process of self-development that can be defined as a Will to Power. This Will is so overpowering that in order to be true to its own nature it somehow begins to reveal itself externally, becoming what we call Nature.

This process is best described through the notion of dialectics or the outworking of becoming. John Vander Hoven defines dialects as: "the notion that the basic principle of logic is not the principle of non-contradiction, 'A' over against 'Non-A', but that a more basic unity exists which includes, and relativizes this opposition."[1] This process is best described as the Spirit looking into the mirror of itself and discovering nature. Nature is part of the Spirit but somehow, it is also distinguished from it. What is happening in the process of dialectics or becoming is that the Spirit is uncovering all the hidden possibilities of what it is not. In other words, the dialectic process is a negative process that over time eliminates all that is not pure Spirit. The outworking of Nature is an obstacle that challenges Spirit into the continual process of becoming aware, in an experiential way, of the fullness of its possibilities.

The becoming of nature evolves into family which becomes the bourgeois. For Hegel, "there is no place for a human subject or ego that transcends theoretical reflection."[2] In other words, there is no room for humanity, it is simply a part of the Spirit and will at some point in time be discarded. Therefore, the Spirit begins to emanate self-alienation, which results in confusion and chaos dividing Spirit from life. From this act of becoming the State is formed (by "State" Hegel does not mean simply "the government" but refers to all social life . . . the community as a whole).[3] However, the State is not the end of the process but simply another part

---

1. Vander Hoven, *Karl Marx*, 8.
2. Vander Hoven, *Karl Marx*, 11.
3. Singer, *Hegel*, 57.

of the evolution of Spirit. Perhaps it is better to say that the Spirit is the outworking of History: Spirit is Becoming.

Hegel's idealism did not survive his death. Yet bits and pieces can be found in the work of Karl Marx, among others. Hegel's aspect of the eternal becoming of history can also be found in later philosophies such as positivism, pragmatism, and existentialism. It defines man as a being who is not fixed, but who is a process of historical self-reflection,[4] the difference being that history is no longer seen as the Spirit; history has been replaced by humanity or even the individual—history becomes irrelevant.

Laplace and Comte

In his work, *The Society of the Future*, H. Van Riessen asked the question, "What does modern man expect from science?" He answers by noting that modern history is dominated by Bacon's (1561–1657) theme "knowledge is power" and Comte's (1798–1857) "know and look ahead." Pierre-Simon LaPlace (1749–1827) is also noted as saying:

We ought then to consider the present state of the universe as the effect of its previous state and as the cause of that which is to follow. An intelligence that, at a given instant, could comprehend all the forces by which nature is animated and the respective situation of the beings that make it up, if moreover it were vast enough to submit these data to analysis, would encompass in the same formula the movements of the greatest bodies of the universe and those of the lightest atoms. For such an intelligence nothing would be uncertain, and the future, like the past, would be open to its eyes.[5]

Van Riessen notes that: "Laplace. . .considers the future determined by the past and present so that, in principle at least, the

---

4. Singer, *Hegel*, 8.
5. Laplace, *Philosophical Essay on Probabilities*, 3.

Fragmentation of Philosophy

future is attainable or explicable to science. This scientific ideal dominated the nineteenth century."[6]

In all of this, knowing the facts about reality is very important because the facts lay the foundation for understanding the future. The facts, as laid out by science, teach us not only the progress of the physical world of Newton but, according to Comte, they form the foundation for the "progress of society through science and technique. Thus, the new way of self-redemption in the nineteenth century becomes the way which science shows the future of society."[7]

Comte's positivism is seen as the outworking of the laws of society which unfold in three stages: the theological stage, in which free play is given to spontaneous fictions admitting of no proof; the metaphysical stage, characterized by the prevalence of personified abstractions or entities; lastly, the positive stage, based upon an exact view of the real facts of the case. The first, though purely provisional, is invariably the point from which we start; the third is the only permanent or normal state; the second has but a modifying or rather a solvent influence, which qualifies it for regulating the transition from the first stage to the third.[8]

Comte's notion of the science of society would be picked up in the nineteenth century and mixed with Darwin's theory of evolution by Karl Marx in Germany. On the other side of the globe the same ideas would be developed into the American notion of manifest destiny by some churchmen while at the same time developing into John Dewey's philosophy of pragmatism.

Positivism is a wonderful way of viewing the world if the world works like Newton's machine universe or the wound-up clock of the deists. Yet in the everyday world of humanity, in any age, the world does not work that way at all because there is freedom. The more freedom that is allowed into a system the more that freedom clogs up the works.

6. Riessen, *Society of the Future*, 23.
7. Riessen, *Society of the Future*, 23.
8. Comte, *General View of Positivism*, 2.

All of these theories rely on precision; and freedom is anything but precise. As Reissen notes:

> The starting point and ideal of positivism thus led to an internal insoluble contradiction. It desires to show the way of self-redemption. To that end, man must first establish his own security and independence in the idea of an impeccable, self-sufficient positive science, wholly free of speculation, based solely upon facts. Such a science supplies knowledge enabling man to control reality, thereby insuring progress and social redemption. The humanistic ideal of science (we might call it speculation) is completely harmonious but excludes freedom. The forced entry of a small dose of freedom disturbs the science ideal.[9]

Kierkegaard

Soren Kierkegaard saw humanity losing its humanity in the wake of the philosophers mentioned above. As he looked at the way people went about their day to day lives, he saw that "Living had become a matter of knowing rather than doing, accumulating information and learning things by rote as opposed to making decisions that bore the stamp of individual passion or conviction."[10] He dedicated his life to exploring ways to bring humanity back to life.

Kierkegaard understood that the new science, and the philosophical aftermath of the philosophers implied the death of man. His work is first and foremost a war against the "dehumanization of man."[11] He was especially vigilant in speaking against Hegel for the simple reason that his philosophy eliminated humanness as having any import in the outworking of the world: Mankind—in the eyes of the scientists and philosophers—is irrelevant and therefore subservient to the Absolute Spirit.

---

9. Riessen, *Society of the Future*, 24.
10. Gardiner, *Kierkegaard*, 38.
11. Zuidema, *Communication and Confrontation*, 150.

Fragmentation of Philosophy

Kierkegaard's chief aim in his work was to try and bring humanity back to the human race. He wanted the human race to embrace its existence instead of simply becoming a part of the machine. It is for this reason that Zuidema writes: "Kierkegaard can be viewed as the spiritual father of modern existentialist philosophy."[12]

Nietzsche

My wife and I have had an ongoing discussion about Nietzsche for as long as I can remember. I was not going to say anything about it, but I left a copy of *The Birth of Tragedy* on the couch and I should have known better. My wife is adamant that if there is no God, she would still be good because, well, that is just the best way to be. No line of argument can persuade her. I admire her for that but that does not mean she is right!

I, on the other hand, stand with Nietzsche. If there is no God, then there is no good or bad or indifferent. The phrase that sums this chapter up is, "Nothing matters and what if it did?" If there is no God there is no order, there is no law, there is no world that we can actually touch or feel. I could go on and on (and if this were a discussion with my wife I probably would).

For me it comes down to this: If I had not put my faith in Christ and understood the radicalness of that leap, I would have embraced Nietzsche; for he clearly saw that anything other than Christ or Anti-Christ was an untenable compromise. Therefore, he chose Anti-Christ. Van Riessen writes that Nietzsche was an "irrationalist. He disqualifies both reason and systematic knowledge. For him philosophy is action. . .he sought something else than a scholarly system, something more than mere reason."[13] I can relate to all of those motives. I understand that God is not a slave to reason, God is not a rationalist. Neither is God an irrationalist.

---

12. Zuidema, *Kierkegaard*, 9.
13. Van Reissen, *Nietzsche*, 10.

However, God is sometimes unreasonable. This is shown in the fact that the human race is allowed continued existence. Reason would demand humans be wiped out and all freedom to choose taken away. Mercy, Grace, and Love are not reasonable in any sense of the word. Thus, Nietzsche and I would both agree that a reasonable faith is not faith at all. Certainly, a reasonable God—would not be able to find a place for either of us in his or her system.

That being said, these days I cannot embrace the notion of a rationalist supreme being. I opt for a non-rationalist God who is bigger than rationalism and reason while at the same time endued with the fullness of life; a God who wants those that would follow to embrace life in its fullness and be doers of the word instead of hearers only. That is exactly what Nietzsche wanted from humanity, he understood the options and chose the Anti-Christ or Dionysius. He thought it better to turn his back on an impotent unbelieving church and struggle against the Christ they proclaimed. With Nietzsche, philosophy made the shift from the nature-freedom religious ground motive where nature is dominant toward the freedom-nature religious ground motive. Freedom is beginning to be the driving force of philosophy.

Van Riessen asks: "What is it that agitates Nietzsche so deeply?" His answer is:

> He is a child of his time, and his time was the calm before the storm. . . . He sees the choice which modern man would face in the coming century; and that he himself makes his choice, courageously, radically and logically—even though his choice meant that he himself, in a sense, must perish.[14]

Nietzsche chose freedom, to the chagrin of the positivists. He chose to become the only thing that can block the road to progress. Why? Because he understood that if there is no God there is no such thing as progress because there is no meaning. With

---

14. Van Reissen, *Nietzsche*, 9.

Fragmentation of Philosophy

Nietzsche the move to embrace meaninglessness began but it did not fully develop until after the storm.

Nietzsche did not have to have ESP in order to sense that the storm was coming. By the time he was seventeen he had already heard of the rumors of war. The land of the free was locked in a struggle of opposing reasons. Both sides professed to enter the war on reasonable grounds. Both sides could logically support their side of the argument.

Here is where Nietzsche's understanding that there are no such things as brute facts comes into play. Both sides took the same information, the same facts and interpreted them from their own perspective. Neither side could counteract the arguments of the other side with reason alone. There was nothing to do but duke it out.

So, by the time Nietzsche was twenty-one, 2 percent of the United States population was dead (a recent study of Civil War casualties based on census records has increased the estimated total deaths from 620,000 to 750,000). In America, the slaughter of human life remained in our consciences deeply enough to ensure that any future conflicts (at least through the twentieth century) would be fought anywhere except the continental USA.

A few years after Nietzsche's death, conflict began in Europe. There was no longer a singular thing known as reason common to everyone. As the Old Testament often says, everyone was doing what was right in their own eyes. The difference here is that only the powerful were able to do what was right in their eyes. Those without power died in the struggle of the powerful.

There were multiple conflicts arising across Europe not long after the turn of the century: the Boxer Rebellion, the Balkan Wars, struggles in Russia, and on a smaller scale struggles worldwide between labor and management. These things were encroaching the edges of Nietzsche's calm. Then on July 28, 1914, the struggle of the powerful began in full force with the First World War.

For this struggle, reason developed new mechanical methods of mass destruction. Four years later something on the order of 9.5 million people from around the world were dead, not including the 15 million who were wounded or the millions of civilians who died. Martin Gilbert writes:

> More than nine million soldiers, sailors and airmen were killed in the First World War. A further five million civilians are estimated to have perished under occupation, bombardment, hunger and disease. The mass murder of Armenians in 1915, and the influenza epidemic that began while the war was still being fought, were two of its destructive by-products. The flight of Serbs from Serbia at the end of 1915 was another cruel episode in which civilians perished in large numbers; so too was the Allied naval blockade of Germany, as a result of which more than three-quarters of a million German civilians died.[15]

Add to that the fallout of the Russian Civil War which "caused the death of an estimated 13.5 million people, almost 10 percent of the population—12 million civilians and 1.5 million soldiers."[16] Unlike the two world wars, however, the Russian Civil War did not spread across Europe or beyond. Rather, it was a struggle for power following the Russian Revolution, and it pitted the Bolsheviks, headed by Lenin, against a coalition called the White Army."[17]

At this point in time, it is probably wise to put those numbers into perspective for our day and age. The death toll of World War I would be equivalent to leveling New York City, Los Angeles County, and all of metro Chicago leaving no survivors. That was only the era of the First World War.

The above statement is for my own benefit, for you see, I am an average American. As a result, I have a skewed view of the history of the twentieth century. Americans did not know that Nietzsche's calm was gone. I was told my entire life that peace was all around me—even though we have been in one conflict or another since before I was born. America has a "don't ask don't tell" policy with regard to war. Though I do not agree with all that Gore Vidal writes I believe his notion of the United States being in

---

15. Gilbert, *First World War*, 5.
16. "The Russian Civil War," *Military History Monthly*.
17. "The Russian Civil War," *Military History Monthly*.

Fragmentation of Philosophy

a "Perpetual War for Perpetual Peace" is pretty much on target.[18] I would probably expand that to say that the nations of the world are doing their best to bring that to reality.

Though the warfare slowed down for the next twenty one years after WWI, it never entirely went away.[19] By 1939 the so-called "war to end all wars" had begun. The Second World War was among the most destructive conflicts in human history; more than forty-six million soldiers and civilians perished, many in circumstances of prolonged and horrifying cruelty. During the 2,174 days of war between the German attack on Poland in September 1939 and the surrender of Japan in August 1945, by far the largest number of those killed, whether in battle or behind the lines, were unknown by name or face except to those few who knew or loved them; yet in many cases, perhaps also numbering in the millions, even those who might in later years have remembered a victim were themselves wiped out.[20] This was Nietzsche's storm. The world would never be the same and neither would philosophy.

Existentialism

The existentialists prize the freedom of human beings above all else. While it is a wonderful thing to aspire to, getting there in a mechanical world of cause and effect is especially difficult. In a bold move by the existentialists, they simply bypass nature and begin with existence. Humans exist. Any theory for how we got here is irrelevant; we are here. Our being is the most important thing. Being is more important than knowing what we are. It is more important than our essence.

The existentialist begins with humans because that is really all a person can know—him or herself. We cannot know if there is an outside world. We cannot know if there is a god. We know that we exist and that we are somehow bound by time and time is

18. Vidal, *Perpetual War for Perpetual Peace*.
19. See the list of major twentieth-century wars: https:/www.thoughtco.com/major-wars-and-conflicts-20th-century- 1779967.
20. Gilbert, *Second World War*, 12.

our enemy. It will eventually bring an end to us. But while we have it, we must be free. We are under no law but our own and must pursue our will regardless of the cost. Why? Because death is coming for us all. Life, even if it is meaningless, is better than death. We exist, if only for a moment, and in that time, we should strive to come to terms with our essence, who we really are. Nothing matters and everything matters and then you die is, at least from my limited perspective, the essence of existentialism.

6

Ignoring Fragmentation —American Pragmatism

THE STRUGGLE TO FIND the heart of Americanism was not solely political; it was a part of a new view of the world that was slowly working its way through every area of life. In studying the development of this new view of the world in America one must begin with an understanding of religion, for America has always been rooted in religion. The question has always been: What religion?

In the early years of the nineteenth century America experienced two religious revivals. The first, which was mentioned in a previous chapter, was known as the Second Great Awakening. The main influence in this revival were preachers such as Charles Finney and Francis Asbury. It primarily impacted poorer, lesser educated parts of the population, though it was not strictly segregated by any means. The movement impacted those who would later call themselves Evangelicals.

The second religious outbreak occurred in more the educated and upper-class areas of society: Especially those who had been raised in the Puritan tradition. This religious awakening was a turn away from Scottish Common Sense Presbyterianism and Puritanism toward transcendentalism and Unitarianism. It was this revival of religion which would dominate America well into the twentieth century.

Background

By the time of the American Revolution both Thomas Jefferson and Benjamin Franklin openly embraced deism, though for many that was a step too far. Atheism was still taboo, and deism was too close to the border for most. In intellectual circles reasonable Christianity was quickly moving away from orthodoxy.

The American intelligencia were being influenced by Romanticism through German philosophers such as Goethe and Schiller, from England via Carlyle and of course by Rousseau, the father of Romanticism. The transcendentalism of Kant was also influential.[1] The new world took these various ideas and transformed them into a typically American movement. Dr. Cornel West calls this move America's evasion of philosophy. We saw the logical outcome of philosophy given the scientific facts of the nature of humans and the world we believe to be there: and we chose to ignore them. Instead, we chose to press on regardless of what the facts said. In doing so, we lengthened the dead-end road, but we refused to take the only road that could possibly bypass the dead end.

Ralph Waldo Emerson's version of American "Transcendentalism has been defined as 'the flowering of the Puritan spirit" though the Puritans would probably disagree.[2] He did not found pragmatism, but he laid the foundation for it. West notes: "Emerson not only prefigures the dominant themes of American pragmatism but, more important, enacts an intellectual style of cultural criticism that permits and encourages American pragmatists to swerve from mainstream European philosophy."[3]

1. Williams, *Horace Mann*, 69.
2. Williams, *Horace Mann*, 69.
3. West, *American Evasion of Philosophy,* 123–38, 141–60.

Ignoring Fragmentation—American Pragmatism

In the early twentieth century, it was called "an intellectual overture to democracy, a belief in the divinity of human nature."[4] This new American religion, passing itself off as philosophy, held as a founding doctrinal faith the notion of the basic goodness of man and his ultimate perfectibility. Gone were the notions of the fall of man, total depravity, and a need for salvation. Rousseau had directed humanity toward the ultimate goodness of man. Locke wrote "that of all the men we meet with, nine parts of ten are what they are, good or evil, useful or not, by their education."[5] In that statement the seed to renounce the theological notion of total depravity was planted. He does not explicitly say such a thing, but the intent of his writing is that education is now to be the source of morality. The followers of Emerson held on to this notion with all their might—despite plenty of evidence to the contrary.

Rise of Unitarianism

In 1782 the first official Unitarian church, King's Chapel, was formed in Boston with James Freeman as its pastor. By 1840, in Massachusetts there were "one hundred thirty-five Unitarian churches as against four hundred and nine Orthodox and congregational churches. . . . All the leading churches of Boston except Old South Church went Unitarian."[6] But it was not just the churches; Harvard was staffed, both in trustees and professors, with Unitarians. So were the financial class, judges, literary men and public officials.[7]

Their focus, however, was not the churches, they had already conquered those, they were out to reform all of society into perfection through the main arm of the new religion—education. It was the Unitarians who ushered Pestalozzian educational ideas into American education.

4. West, *American Evasion of Philosophy*, 123–38, 141–60.
5. Locke, *John Locke Collection*, loc. 18030–31.
6. Williams, *Horace Mann*, 72, 205.
7. Williams, *Horace Mann*, 72, 205.

Louder Than Words

Pestalozzi

The ideas of Rousseau greatly impacted John Heinrich Pestalozzi (1746–1827). It was he who laid the foundation for what became known as the common school movement in America (later known as public school). Pestalozzi's writings have been described as: "awakening the modern world . . . to a faith in the school as the supreme instrument for saving man from misery and prostration due to his own ineptitude."[8] As an educator he was an abject failure. Every school he started failed. But as the developer of the fundamental principles of a new and modern understanding of education his written discourses were the foundation for educational reform around the world.

He began with three fundamental principles: 1) All genuine reform must begin with the individual and not society. 2) The individual can be elevated only by putting into his grasp the power of helping himself—teach him to help and respect himself. 3) The only means of attaining the end desired is through the process of development through education.[9]

For Pestalozzi, these fundamental principles were to be developed organically in the whole student which was understood in a tripartite manner: the head (the intellect), the hand (the physical) and the heart (the ethical/spiritual). The goal is to empower the student to do what is taught and not just know what is taught. He writes: "To know what is right and what is best, unless it is combined with the will and capacity to act accordingly, can only be a source of weakness; it is in fact rather a hindrance than a help."[10]

As a result of his writings on education Pestalozzi "democratized education by proclaiming that it is the absolute right of every child to have his God given powers fully developed."[11] In doing so he furthered the Romantic notion of the natural goodness of

---

8. Eby and Arrowood, *Development of Modern Education*, 619.
9. Eby and Arrowood, *Development of Modern Education*, 636.
10. Green, *Life and Work of Pestalozzi*, 348–49.
11. Eby and Arrowood, *Development of Modern Education*, 663.

mankind and further elevated education as the means of saving mankind from its wretched environment.

Horace Mann

Horace Mann (1796–1859) led the way in founding Pestalozzi's common school approach to education in America. Mann understood that "true religion would be best served by the school, and that the churches were in error in their interpretation of their faith and its realm."[12] Mann was on the front lines of the shift of American Christianity from the Scottish Common Sense Philosophy-based Presbyterianism toward the anthropology-based Christianity rooted in Enlightenment and Romantic understandings of the world.

Williams notes that Mann, "a thorough believer in the 'perfectibility of man,' saw the school as an institution which would regenerate society."[13] Mann expressed his views before an audience of educators saying:

> I believe in the existence of a great, immortal, immutable principle of natural law or natural ethics—a principle antecedent to all human institutions, and incapable of being abrogated by any ordinance of man,—a principle of divine origin, clearly legible in the ways of providence as those ways are clearly manifested in the order of nature and in the history of the race, which proves the absolute right to an education of every human being that comes into the world; and which, of course, proves the correlative duty of every government to see the means of education are provided for all.[14]

Mann wrote in his work, *What God Does and What He Leaves for Man to Do in the Work of Education*:

---

12. Rushdoony, *Messianic Character of American Education*, 18.
13. Williams, *Horace Mann*, 205.
14. Mann, *Life and Works of Horace Mann*, vol. 2, 115–16.

> With our Revolution, the current of human events was turned quite round, and set upon a new course. That external power which, theretofore, had palsied the propensities of the mass, was abolished. Instead of the old axiom, that the ruler is a lord,—a vicegerent of God,—here, to a proverb, rulers are servants. Lightly and fearfully the law lays its hand upon men; and, should the wisest law ever framed chafe the passions or propensities of the majority, or of men who can muster a majority, they speak, and the law perishes. The will of the people must be our law, whether that will reads the moral code forwards or backwards.[15]

Mann's ideas were more steeped in transcendental Unitarianism than in the Bible. Humanity is downgraded in Mann's eyes and his understanding of kings and rulers as God's vicegerents is also not biblical. From a biblical perspective all human beings were to be God's vicegerents over the Earth.[16] They lost that privilege when they rebelled against God's authority. For Mann, the problem with man is not sin; it is his instincts and his indulgences, nothing that proper education cannot overcome.

With regard to the sovereignty of God, Mann expresses his perspective when he wrote:

> Now for the great end of ransoming the human race from its brutish instincts and its demoniac indulgences, let us see what the benevolence of God does for us, in the common course of nature and providence, and what His wisdom has left for us to do;—because it is obvious, that He may go on doing his part of the work, for a hundred, or for a thousand generations, and yet, unless we also do our part, the work will never get done. And it may be further remarked that while He does His part, and we neglect ours, the work, so far from being half done, will be worse than undone. But His part of the work—that is,

---

15. Mann, *Life and Works of Horace Mann*, vol. 2, 196.
16. See Schrotenboer, "Man in God's World," Wolters, *Creation Regained*.

Ignoring Fragmentation—American Pragmatism

the general course of nature and providence,—will go on whether we cooperate or not.[17]

His notion of God seems to be anything but biblical as he limits God to directing the general course of nature and providence. In many ways, his God is simply the machine of Newton. However, according to Mann time is on our side. Why? Because God, the controller of nature, is waiting on us for his will to be done in our area of expertise. He is powerless to act unless we act.

In this understanding of God, we find the idea behind manifest destiny and the idealism of Hegel. This was the spirit of the age throughout the latter half of the nineteenth and early part of the twentieth century. With persuasive words and the "science" of education as its tools; pragmatic education slowly began evolving into one of the inalienable rights given in America's Declaration of Independence.

Mann and other early common school proponents held that if citizens were going to be able to participate in a democracy they needed to be enlightened through a free system of education. In early to mid-nineteenth century education was generally restricted to the upper classes. For Mann education was seen as the great leveler of society. For democracy to succeed common school education must succeed, at least that was the understanding at the time. As a result, what is now known as public education slowly began to take a greater hold in America with each passing year. The direction it would lead began to take a radical turn in 1859 when Charles Darwin published *The Origin of Species*.

G. Stanley Hall

When Darwin's classic work was published the renowned educator, G. Stanley Hall, was thirteen years old. Hall, "coming to manhood in the time of Darwin and of Huxley, found his escape from the rigidity of Puritan orthodoxy in an ecstatic acceptance of the mystery and the beauty and the far-reaching possibilities of the theory

---

17. Mann, *Life and Works of Horace Mann*, vol. 2, 199.

Louder Than Words

of evolution."[18] Ebby noted that in Darwin's work "every subject of human interest came in gradually for complete re-organization in light of this new point of view. One of the most difficult problems that faced the theory of evolution was to account for the human mind and soul."[19] It was this reconciliation that became the focus of Hall's life. "He strove to understand the history of the mind that he might understand the possibilities of the single child. . . . He was a crusading knight, riding to the rescue of the distressed, and he was able to enlist countless others under the banner that proclaimed the ideal of a wholesome and happy child."[20]

Through his research and study, Hall developed the concept that the human race was to be understood in terms of the child through the lens of evolution and the primitive past.[21] As a result, in both education and the culture at large the child slowly became the father to the man. Children were to be served by society, so much so that there could be no room for delinquent children, only delinquent parents and educators. The child is the norm. His greatness is his closeness to the race's primitive past, and his future lies in his affirmation of those primitive roots, the pathway of progress lies in the primitive, looking backwards to Eden; a concept aptly reformatted in Joni Mitchell's song "Woodstock."

The crowning achievement of Hall's work was his development of the concept of adolescence—the transition from child to adult—from primitive past into the new Eden. The evolutionary pathway "rightly and broadly interpreted gave a new basis for democracy and government for and by the people."[22] The equations of childhood and adolescence with the primitive past would come to fruition in the decades to come. As a result, American society would have to deal with scientific racism's notion that first, the so-called black race was more primitive than the white race, and second, the embrace of adolescent whites of the primitive music

18. Pruette, *G. Stanley Hall*, 207.
19. Eby and Arrowood, *Development of Modern Education*, 843.
20. Eby and Arrowood, *Development of Modern Education*, 845.
21. Rushdoony, *Messianic Character*, 126.
22. Hall, *Life and Confessions of a Psychologist*, 363.

Ignoring Fragmentation—American Pragmatism

of blacks. In doing so, a generation of adolescents raised in accordance with Hall's teaching would embrace fully what they had been taught, to the chagrin of the community leaders who had been taught differently. However, before those things developed, a student of G. Stanley Hall's, John Dewey (1859–1952), would have to place his stamp upon American public education.

John Dewey

In the book *Development of Modern Education* published in 1934 the authors proclaim: "For thirty years Dr. John Dewey has been one of the foremost educational leaders in America."[23] Dewey, writing toward the end of his life, could look back upon the progress of the common school movement and write with pride: "On the side of the mechanical and the external . . . the immediate ideals of Horace Mann and the others have been realized."[24]

Dewey's work shifted the educational focus from the individual in society to a socialized individual as a part of a group; the end being the individual finding his or her place within the social structure for the good of society. For Dewey education is a social process "securing direction and development in the immature through their participation in the life of the group to which they belong."[25] In fact, for Dewey "the moral trinity of the school" was "social intelligence, social power, and social interests."[26]

It is this social aspect of the American education system which is most important in the present study. Yet the concept of the social nature of education is not the sole import of Dewey's ideas of education. Dewey's notion of socialization also includes a strong emphasis on the individual. Certainly, the individual is shaped by the group but at the same time the individual shapes the group. For Dewey, "true individualism is a product of the

23. Eby and Arrowood, *Development of Modern Education*, 855.
24. Dewey, *Problems of Men*, loc. 545–48
25. Dewey, *John Dewey Premium Collection*, loc. 1402.
26. Dewey, *Moral Principles of Education*, loc. 10894.

relaxation of the grip of the authority of custom and traditions as standards of belief."[27] History within an overarching worldview is of no import. History is only important as it can be used to direct the individual to become all they can be for the good of the group.

The consequences of the thinking espoused by Dewey in 1916 (the year before America entered World War I) would not be completely worked out in lives until the 1950s. In an intellectual vacuum perhaps Dewey's vision, of group socialization and individualism free from the customs and mores of history, would have been a wonderful sight to behold. However, there is no such thing as an intellectual or educational vacuum, and the unfolding of history rooted in customs and mores dramatically put an end to Dewey's vision: first with the Industrial Revolution and then two world wars.

In his last book published while he was alive (six years before his death), *The Problems of Men*, Dewey wrote: "The cleavage in life that has been brought about by "modern" departures from and revolt against older practices and tenets is so widespread that nothing is left untouched."[28] Dewey could look back and see that his work had accomplished much. And yet, throughout the book he continually expressed frustration that his ideas had not been taken any further. Humanity had yet to be scientifically transformed into a new humanity. But Americans had been transformed. Individualism came to the forefront. Pragmatism, whatever seems to work, became the foundation for life. Industry was pragmatic, the church became pragmatic, education was pragmatic, families became pragmatic. The problem was pragmatism coupled with American individualism opened the door to the "I, Me, Mine" culture. The result was that pragmatism did not avert the spread of existentialist angst and fragmentation that Europe had embraced during the early twentieth century; it only postponed it for a generation. It began to grow in the cracks of individuals struggling to retain a semblance of unity. By the 1950s it began to explode in almost every area of life. America responded with increased pragmatism

---

27. Dewey, *Democracy and Education*, loc. 4972–74.
28. Dewey, *Problems of Men*. loc. 88–89.

Ignoring Fragmentation—American Pragmatism

and the result has been an ever increasing, though rather slow, expansion of the fragmentation of life.

7

Fragmentation of Humanity: Part 1

SOMETIME IN THE 1950S a television crew recorded the following comments from two members of the Alabama White Citizens Committee. The executive secretary said, "The obscenity and vulgarity of rock and roll music is obviously a means by which the white man and his children can be driven to a level with the nigger." The chairman of that committee added: "We have set up a 20 member committee to do away with this vulgar, animalistic, nigger, rock and roll bop."[1] Also, during this same time period another man was filmed saying: "They can send the FBI and the army to force us white people, here in St. Augustine and other parts of the nation, to mix up with niggers. . .whether he sends troops in here and puts a bayonet behind every one of us we will still not mix with a bunch of black savages."[2]

One certainly can hear stories of racism from that time period and have an intellectual understanding of those times but there is something about seeing and hearing men in the context of the time—full of anger and fear—say words which chill one to the bone.

1. Axelrod, *History of Rock 'n' Roll*, Disc 1 episode 2 section 1.
2. Axelrod, *History of Rock 'n' Roll*, Disc 1 episode 2 Section 11.

Fragmentation of Humanity: Part 1

In the following chapter I will begin by defining racism. From there I will briefly explore the history and development of the modern slave trade and from that foundation trace the development of racism in America from its inception until the late 1950s. By the early fifties, segregation in America was at the beginning of the end. In 1954 the Supreme Court, with its landmark case of *Brown vs. the Board of Education*, declared that segregation of students in public schools violated the fourteenth amendment.[3] It was the end of an almost hundred-year journey which grew out of the institution of slavery and had been a part of America's history since before its beginning as a nation. In fact, before there was a push for democracy in America there was a push for slavery.

Definition

To understand the nature of the problem we must begin with a definition of exactly what racism is. It is more than simply not liking another person or group of persons—the history of the world is filled with conflicts between people groups. Racism begins with a premise that is thoroughly non-biblical: There is a hierarchy of worth in the human race.

Taken to extremes this thought process can lead to the belief that there were multiple creations which gave us multiple races or from a Darwinian perspective, different people groups exhibit differing degrees of evolutionary development. The Bible is clear that human beings are all one blood (Acts 17:26) or to put it another way: one race—the human race. In fact, one of the early building blocks of the foundation of western culture was that the work of Christ provided grace to any human being who would receive it. Coupled with that was the understanding that all "who were baptized into Christ have clothed themselves with Christ. There is neither Jew nor Greek, there is neither slave nor free, there is neither male nor female; for you are all one in Christ Jesus" (Gal 3:27–28).

---

3. Encyclopedia Brittanica, "Brown vs. the Board of Education," https://www.britannica.com/event/Brown-v-Board-of-Education-of-Topeka.

But of course, humanity is rather ingenious when it comes to finding loopholes in almost every situation.

George M. Frederickson, professor of United States history at Stanford and author of several books on American racism, gives this definition of racism: it is "more than a theory about human differences or thinking badly of a group over which one has no control. It either directly sustains or proposes to establish a racial order, a permanent group hierarchy that is believed to reflect the laws of nature or the decrees of God."[4] The question, which no one ever seems to ask, is which God is Fredrickson referring to? The assumption is usually the God of the Bible. However, as there is no establishment of a racial order in the Bible, so where does such an understanding come from?

The answer is to be found in the work of the medieval scholar Thomas Aquinas, the father of Christian scholasticism. Writing in the thirteenth century his thought processes led to the development of his magnum opus, *Summa Theologica*, which laid the foundation of Christian thought through the modern and into the postmodern age. The background of Aquinas's work in using the Platonic notion of the great chain of being was noted in a previous chapter. What follows is the history of the development of that hierarchy within those who have human form.

The first evidence of such a tendency in western culture appeared with regard to the Jews. In the fourteenth century the Black Death ravaged Europe, killing millions. Rumors began to spread that the plague was caused by the Jews who had poisoned the wells with an eye toward destroying the Christian culture of the West. As the lie spread, so too, did outbreaks of riotous acts of violence against the Jews. This was not yet racism but more of an attitude of persecution. During this time European Christendom showed increasing hostility to three groups—Jews, heretics, and lepers. R. I. Moore notes that the culture of the time facilitated "the assimilation of Jews, heretics and lepers into a single rhetoric . . . depicting

---

4. Fredrickson, *Racism: A Short History*, 8.

them as a single though many-headed threat to the security of the Christian order."⁵

Throughout the passage of time, the attitude in the western world toward the Jews only degenerated. "That Jews were possessed of the spirit of perversity and stubbornness the medieval mind did not doubt. But whence came that spirit? How was it that the psychology of the Jews should be contrary to all human experience? The answer was that the Jew was not human—not in the sense that the Christian was. He was a creature of an altogether different nature, of whom normal human reactions could not be expected."⁶ L. A. Williams quotes Peter the Venerable of Cluny as saying, "Really I doubt whether a Jew can be human for he will neither yield to human reasoning, nor find satisfaction in authoritative utterances, alike divine and Jewish."⁷

Precursor to Racism

It is at this point that we begin to see for the first time a hierarchy in the order of creation: Some people are less than human and as a result are unredeemable. They are in fact in league with the devil.

> It was not, therefore, that the Jews did not believe in Christianity, in the same sense as Moslems or heathens did not believe it. It was that they were constitutional antagonists of Jesus Christ—of a Jesus whom they knew to have existed and to have been justified in his Divine claims, but whom they crucified rather than admit being their king. . .The Jews then deliberately rejected Christianity, while realizing the full the implications of their attitude. . .Conscious misbelievers such as these were plainly less than human. Individuals whose whole life was a perpetual conflict against Jesus and his followers were capable of any crime, imaginable or unimaginable.⁸

---

5. Moore, *Formation of a Persecuting Society*, 88.
6. Trachtenberg, *Devil and the Jews*, loc. 458.
7. Trachtenberg, *Devil and the Jews*, loc 2758.
8. Roth, *Essential Papers*, 307–8.

The situation was somewhat different in Spain during the Middle Ages. It was known as the Spain of "the Three Religions, [Christian, Jew, and Muslim] where all the religions were respected, changing from one religion to another, even converting to Christianity, was either forbidden or made very difficult. The exercise of each religion was officially protected by the government and even regulated by it."[9] It is in Spain that the Christians and Jews worked together to translate Aristotle and various other works of philosophy from Arabic. Jews would translate the books into Castilian and then the Christians would translate those works into Latin. Jews became extremely important and influential in the courts of the various regions within Spain.

Eventually, however, the Christian forces in Spain turned their attention to removing Muslims from the Iberian Peninsula. By 1492, the Reconquista, as it was called, came to an end with the signing of the treaty of Granada. Muslims had effectively been removed from Spain. At first, the Reconquista focused only on Muslims while the Jews were left in relative peace. However, as the fourteenth century unfolded, anti-Jewish attitudes began to develop and soon spread throughout the Iberian Peninsula; toward the end of the century most Spanish communities were seeing pogroms, even massacres of Jews.

Whether of true faith or to keep their status in society, it is hard to say, but many Jews began to convert to Christianity. They were called *conversos* and they were seen as second-class Christians at best. Such a move bought a limited amount of time for Jews. By 1449, in the city of Toledo, the city officials proclaimed that all *conversos* were unfit to hold public or private office, to be witnesses or notaries and to hold any authority over Old Christians. They were too corrupt by nature to be true Christians.

---

9. Poliakov, *History of Anti-Semitism*, 122.

Fragmentation of Humanity: Part 1

Tainted Blood

In the sixteenth century the leaders of the Spanish Inquisition developed the concept of *limpieza de sangre*, the purity of the blood which was another subtle outworking of the hierarchy of those with human form. Fredrickson writes: "Sixteenth- and seventeenth-century Spain is critical to the history of western racism because its attitudes and practices served as a kind of segue between the religious intolerance of the Middle Ages and the naturalistic racism of the modern era. [At this time] the idiom remained religious, and what was inherited through the 'blood' was a propensity to heresy or unbelief rather than intellectual or emotional inferiority."[10] They were lower on the hierarchy and therefore had less capacity to be spiritual and possessed a deeper material and unholy tendency.

Slavery

As noted previously, Christians and Jews had worked together to translate from Arabic the works of Aristotle into both Castilian and Latin. It was this "revival and rediscovery of classical learning—supposedly a liberating step toward progress—[that] gave new support for slavery in the Renaissance" with the Aristotelian concept of a "natural slave."[11] In his work *Politics*, Aristotle concludes that "Where then there is such a difference as that between soul and body, or between men and animals (as in the case of those whose business is to use their body, and who can do nothing better), the lower sort are by nature slaves, and it is better for them as for all inferiors that they should be under the rule of a master."[12]

In 1550–51, Juan Ginés Sepúlveda used Aristotle's theory of slavery as the basis for his debate with Bartolomé de Las Casas, arguing that "the American Indians had been created to be natural slaves (with Las Casas attacking that conclusion but not Aristotle's

---

10. Fredrickson, *Racism: A Short History*, 40.
11. Davis, *Inhuman Bondage,* loc. 1811.
12. Aristotle, *Complete Aristotle.* loc. 36784.

basic premises)."[13] Sepúlveda's point of view would hold sway for the next five hundred years.

It is important to understand that Aristotle's natural slave,

> "Was not literally seen as an animal but as a subhuman who lacks the higher powers of reason and imaginative judgment to govern and balance such animalistic functions as eating, sleeping, defecating, and, above all, mating— the things we share with animals, often with a touch of embarrassment and with a strong counter drive to 'elevate' and 'civilize' our behavior and that of people around us. Hence in the classical Greek tradition, the slavish person would be ideally suited to perform all the menial, unpleasant, and degrading labor that made the civilized state possible, providing 'citizens' with the freedom and leisure needed for the so-called good life."[14]

Slavery before the New World

Slavery had long been the practice of the day, it just so happened that before the discovery of the New World, slaves were primarily white. In fact, from the early sixteenth century into the nineteenth century Moorish slave traders showed no qualms about enslaving over a million "whites."[15] We must understand that

> The European approach to racial slavery was unplanned, haphazard, and long barred by the formidable Islamic control of North Africa, by the vast Sahara desert, and by the availability of diverse populations of white or tan "infidel" slaves (including some Eastern Christians as well as Muslims). . .Barbary corsairs continued to enslave white Europeans and Americans well into the nineteenth century. . .It was not until the seventeenth century that New World slavery began to be overwhelmingly associated

---

13. Davis, *Inhuman Bondage,* loc. 1303-1305.
14. Davis, *Inhuman Bondage,* loc. 1308-1313.
15. Davis, *Inhuman Bondage,* loc. 1811.

with people of black African descent— as opposed to Native Americans and whites.[16]

It was only after the Muslim takeover of Constantinople in 1453 by the Ottoman Turks that white slave trade ended in the western world. The Turk victory blocked "the entrance from the Mediterranean into the Black Sea. The Turks soon diverted the flow of Black Sea and Balkan captives solely to Islamic markets. Turkish expansion . . . cut off Christian Europe from its major source of slaves, and for most potential buyers the price of slaves became prohibitive. Aside from captured Muslims, the only alternative [before the discovery of the New World] . . . was sub-Saharan Africa."[17]

More Non-Biblical Christian Justification

However, the New World was discovered. Not long after the Turkish blockade to the east was set in place, Christopher Columbus, at the behest of King Ferdinand and Queen Isabella of Spain, mistakenly discovered the New World while searching for an alternative route around the blockade and as a result he discovered a new people whom he called Indians. By 1495, Columbus had transported some four or five hundred so-called Indians back to Spain as slaves.

Though there was some talk about the Native Americans being a part of the so-called lost tribes of Israel, ultimately, they were seen as being neither Spanish nor Christian, therefore purity of blood was not an issue: their blood was impure. What we find then is that for the Spanish, "in America, the skin, more or less white, is what dictates the class that an individual occupies in society. A white, even if he rides barefoot on horseback, considers himself to be a member of the nobility of the country."[18] It is here, in the New World, where skin color was for the first time used to classify

---

16. Davis, *Inhuman Bondage*, loc. 1265-71.
17. Davis, *Inhuman Bondage*, loc. 1888-93.
18. Morner, *Race Mixture*, 55-56.

people of a country. Up to this time period it was still believed that skin color differences were largely due to the effects of climate on humans over the course of a few centuries. Blacks were black because they lived in tropical areas. Whites were white because they lived in temperate areas. In the sixteenth century there was a yearning for Europeans to explore and conquer the world but if whites thought they might eventually turn black when they went to the tropics, well, they probably would not go.

In 1578 George Best tried to encourage western expansion to other regions of the world by putting forth the concept that racial type was fixed and impervious to physical environment as the theory of the biblical curse of Ham seemed to declare. Whites therefore should have no fear of turning black and blacks, therefore, could be seen as permanently consigned to slavery.[19] In 1602, the biblical concept of the curse of Ham was developed further by "the great Jewish philosopher and statesman Isaac ben Abravanel, [who] having seen many black slaves both in his native Portugal and in Spain, merged Aristotle's theory of natural slaves with the belief that the biblical Noah had cursed and condemned to slavery both his son Ham and his young grandson Canaan. Abravanel concluded that the servitude of animalistic black Africans should be perpetual."[20]

This new "biblically based" idea eased Christian consciences and created a God-given purpose for slavery. Soon blacks were the primary commodity of the slave trade. From that point to the nineteenth century the biblical curse of Ham (sometimes Canaan or even Cain) coupled with the underlying notion of the great chain of being, was used as justification for the enslavement of blacks—Providence had consigned them to slavery, therefore that is the way it had to be. "To a considerable extent, the un-reversible curse of Ham, like the literal demonization of the Jews, operated on the level of popular belief and mythology rather than as formal ideology."[21]

19. Fredrickson, *Racism: A Short History*, 44.
20. Schorsch, *Jews and Black*, 17–22, 27, 36–49.
21. Fredrickson, *Racism: A Short History*, 45.

Fragmentation of Humanity: Part 1

What we see in all of this is a picture of a church that has begun to interpret the Scriptures according to individual whims on a non-biblical foundation. It has become a law unto itself and uses Scripture for its own best interests. The truth is that the "curse of Ham" doctrine had been refuted by leaders in the church who simply noted "that the curse fell on Canaan specifically and not on his brother Cush, who, according to the standard biblical exegesis of sixteenth and seventeenth centuries, was the actual progenitor of the African Race."[22]

These misconstrued biblical notions of Ham and Cain still find adherents in the twenty-first century. I remember being absolutely shocked when I heard the neighbor of a friend start espousing such notions in casual conversation at the turn of the twenty-first century. It was so against anything I had ever understood about Scripture, but this man believed it on the same level that he believed Christ rose from the dead.

A Shift in Worldview

As long as slavery was condoned by society at large, the biblical curse of Ham was enough to justify what was in the hearts of the people. By the "late seventeenth-century, Virginia passed a series of laws that made it clear that conversion did not entail freedom."[23] No longer was it heathenism that allowed one to be enslaved but simply having ancestors that were heathen: never mind that at one time white Europeans were heathens themselves. This shift opened the door to the use of the *limpieza de sangre* (impurity of the blood) concept that had been applied to Jews in Spain now applied to blacks.

Yet, there was another problem. During the same time period a change was occurring in Christianity—the Puritans were on the decline while at the same time groups such as the Quakers, the Anabaptists, and the Unitarians were on the rise. Slavery was

---

22. Fredrickson, *Racism: A Short History*, 45.
23. Fredrickson, *Racism: A Short History*, 45.

becoming a thorn in the side of these new branches of Christianity as well as in those who still held on to the older scholastic orthodox understanding of Scripture. It was understood in some circles that "a person of faith should be the slave of no one but God himself, the chattel servitude of a genuine believer could be troubling."[24]

Using Scripture to justify slavery was becoming a bit of a problem. The gospel was meant to transform the lives of any human being who would humble himself before God. There was one race—the human race that all shared one blood. Such a noteworthy belief was transforming western culture as a whole. By the late eighteenth century, the French and American revolutions were, in theory, overthrowing social hierarchies amongst whites. By all appearances, the playing field was being leveled. In the early years of the nineteenth century, Andrew Jackson leveled the field even more with his presidency of the common man which resulted in a further democratization of the still young America.

These shifts toward an egalitarian view of the human race began to put pressure on the slave trade. In 1807 William Wilberforce succeeded, after twenty-six years of trying, to pass the Abolition of the Slave Trade Act which abolished the slave trade in the British Empire. While the passage of the act abolished the slave trade it did not abolish slavery. It would be twenty-six more years before slavery would be abolished in the British Empire . . . three days before the death of Wilberforce.

The world was changing. So too was America, though in a radically different direction. With the rejection of a biblically based legitimacy for slavery, racism was freed from its constraints, and it began to pursue other means of legitimacy. For that, American slave owners turned to the highest authority of the age of enlightenment—science. They kept the notion of the great chain of being but gradually they began to remove its religious connotations.

Eventually, it would become the foundation for Charles Darwin's theory of evolution but in the mid to late eighteenth-century men like Carl Linnaeus and Johan Fredrick Blumenbach began to classify the human race according to skin color. While they

24. Fredrickson, *Racism: A Short History*, 46.

Fragmentation of Humanity: Part 1

may have held that there was a single human race, it was a race that began with Caucasians from "which all others had diverged or degenerated."[25] In doing so they opened the door to secular or scientific classification of human beings as nothing more than an extension of the animal kingdom in opposition to seeing humanity as made in the image of God and set apart from all other creatures.

It is important to understand that the Neoclassical conceptions of beauty that prevailed in eighteenth century Europe and America were based primarily upon Greek and Roman statuary; the milky whiteness of marble, the facial features and bodily form of Apollo and Venus that were coming to light during the seventeenth and eighteenth centuries through the work of the new scientific field of archeology created a standard of beauty from which Africans were bound to deviate.[26]

By the early nineteenth century ethnological discussion, especially in France, was focused on the debate between a single genesis and polygenesis. Were human beings of one blood or three to five species created at separate times leading to multiple races of differing abilities and capacities? Because of the rise of Evangelical Christianity in England and America, polygenesis of the evolutionary kind was not seriously considered until the mid-nineteenth century.

However, by the 1850s polygenesis had developed substantial credibility in scientific circles. The American school of ethnology provided vast amounts of "scientific" evidence to show that the three races in America, white, black, and Native American (conveniently ignoring the three million Asians who had immigrated to America by this time) were of distinctly different origins: classified as separate but unequal creations.

This pre-Darwinian scientific racism flourished in both France and America more than other areas, probably because these two nations were the most adamant about the natural rights of man and the concept of equality for all citizens. In order to deny full citizenship to blacks and Native Americans, there needed to

---

25. Fredrickson, *Racism: A Short History*, 57.
26. Fredrickson, *Racism: A Short History*, 59–60.

be a distinction between them and white European males. They needed to be viewed as less than human in some sense, biologically unfit to be citizens. This understanding of the law toward blacks and Native Americans was in some sense a continuation of the attitude that excluded women from full citizenship because they were unfit. All were denied equality under the law because they were deemed subhuman or incompetent to fully use the rights of democratic citizenship. It should also be noted that before 1830 not even all white males were qualified to be full citizens and have the right to vote.

The presumption of the inferiority of blacks was not restricted to the southern United States. "The Northern image of the free Negro as a social danger came into sharper focus as time went on."[27] During the early nineteenth century the main solution proposed for the "black problem" in the United States was colonization. This movement sought to send blacks "anywhere but here." In 1820 the American Colonization Society helped free blacks establish the nation of Liberia on the west coast of Africa. Though colonization was a popular idea, the cost of relocating an entire population and settling them in a new community ended up being prohibitive. The idea remained popular until shortly after the Civil War when Abraham Lincoln's proposal to relocate blacks in Panama did not materialize because of the tremendous costs involved.

Ideological Shifts

By the 1830s a radical shift began to take place in the foundation of Christian theology from a synthesis with Enlightenment Rationalism to a synthesis with Romanticism. This shift began to transform the way many viewed the "slave problem." As a result, a new opposition to slavery began to be formed in the North.

> The rise of the abolitionist . . . was a sign that conservative, Neofederalist philanthropy [associated with colonization] was going out of fashion and that Christian

---

27. Fredrickson, *Black Image*, 5.

> reformers were now looking beyond the corporate hierarchical society of the federalists and Calvinists to reforms that reflected new aspirations for the liberation of the individual from the historical and institutional limitations taken for granted by conservatives.[28]

During this time, there was a feeling of newly spun religion of freedom and emotion, ultimately rooted not in Christianity but in Unitarianism, that the millennial kingdom of which Christ spoke was now within sight. The concept of "manifest destiny" began to take on new meaning, leaving behind the determinism associated with Rationalism, rooted in Enlightenment philosophy, disguised as the work of John Calvin, and leading the country forward by vox populi vox dei. It was now the people of God embodying the sovereign will by their push for "Christian" reform in every area of life that would bring about the millennial kingdom.

Education became the new method of salvation. Man was no longer under the thumb of the depravity of the human soul but rather anyone who wanted could be saved. Perfection could be taught. Sin could be abolished by sheer force of will. The kingdom could be brought to fruition by the hard work of humanity, almost instantaneously, if we would only work together. Those who refused to rid America of its societal ills by their own free will would simply be forced to do so. The kingdom of God (made in man's image) was coming—even if it meant a war between the states.

With the religious shift of the American North the so-called religious foundations for the enslavement of blacks began to lose their validity. In order to maintain their way of life, which was still rooted primarily in the Christian rationalism of the pre-Romantic age, the southern states seceded from the Union and formed the Confederacy. While the slavery problem was initially seen as the main thrust of the war, it was not long before that shifted to the unity of the American nation, and for some the goal became nothing more than the destruction of the south for what they had done to the nation.

---

28. Fredrickson, *Black Image*, 27.

Before the Civil War between the states began, Nathaniel Hawthorne wrote of proponents on both sides, "All are thoroughly in earnest, and all pray for the blessings of heaven to rest upon the enterprise. The appeals are so numerous, fervent, and yet so contradictory, that the Great Arbitrator to whom they so piously and solemnly appeal must be sorely puzzled how to decide."[29]

Both sides were praying for a short and decisive battle, but that Great Arbitrator answered both with a resounding "No!" The Civil War between the states was longer and bloodier than anyone had dreamed possible. The country was filled with a bitter suffering. At the same time vengeance for that suffering was taken out by the victors upon the losers.

A few of the victors were looking forward to the implementation of justice and equality for the freedmen as the goal of the war effort. However, "for a larger number of loyal Northerners the question of Negro rights was, from first to last, clearly subordinate to the more fundamental aim of ensuring national hegemony for Northern political, social, and economic institutions."[30] It was with this in mind that the reconstruction of the South began in earnest.

Reconciliation

Time is a factor in the outcome of any venture. Do those who have the desire to implement new ideology have the strength of character to see their venture through to the end? As with the war itself, those who took on the task of reconstruction underestimated the amount of time, effort, and money such an undertaking would require. The effort to bring the Southern states under Republican hegemony was certainly valiant. The Reconstructionists brought about the passage of the fourteenth amendment of the constitution which provided citizenship for all persons born or naturalized in the United States and passage of the fifteenth amendment ensuring voting rights for all citizens, as well as other Reconstructionist

---

29. Hawthorne, *Selected Letters*, 239.
30. Fredrickson, *Black Image*, 165.

laws—all of which laid the foundation of a more egalitarian governance of the people of the United States. However, passage of such laws is one thing, implementation of said laws is quite another. Reconstruction began in 1863 and was eventually implemented with the help of federal troops. However, some fourteen years later when an act of congress forced the withdrawal of the troops from the South, reconstruction came to an end.

8

Fragmentation of Humanity: Part 2

IN EXAMINING THE CONCEPT of race, we cannot restrict our study to that of blacks. The human race is not obviously segregated into black and white. In fact, when it comes to the topic of races the process of defining what was truly "white" is a long and laborious process. In America in the late eighteenth century the British were having a problem with the colonists who lived in the nether regions between the landed gentlemen and the Native Americans.

These colonists, known locally as "crackers", were apparently a significant problem for the British colonial authorities, who were at pains not to agitate the Cherokee to whom they had promised an end to British colonial expansion. "Crackers" were people who lived off the land (owned by other people) hunting, fishing, sometimes stealing in order to survive. They were viewed by the British as people of deplorable habits and moral disrepute. In garnering such a reputation, they were placed into the same unfavorable category as black servants, slaves, and Native Americans. This sub-human who rested on the lowest rung on the ladder of the great chain of being was viewed by those who rested on higher rungs with deep aversion. They were characterized as being dirty, smelly, unclean, immoral, and lazy.

Fragmentation of Humanity: Part 2

While those who placed themselves above the "crackers" held them in disdain, they had no problem using them to their own ends. One thing "we do know without a doubt is that poor whites made up the majority of those who served—willingly and unwillingly—in the militias and armies that repelled the British forces during the war. Yet despite their service to the new nation, in the wake of the revolution poor whites were again marked off as inferior and unworthy whites—as social outcasts whose possible roles in and contributions to the newly formed nation were deeply questioned."[1]

Poor White Trash

Sometime in the early nineteenth century blacks coined a new term for these whites who seemed to have it worse off than they did. It was simultaneously a term of pity and of scorn. To blacks these downtrodden whites were simply known as poor white trash. To the upper crusted whites this term helped clarify a social boundary identifying those "whites who did not rise or live up to their ideals of industry, laboring not at all, or only in the most degrading jobs toiling beneath or alongside the slaves."[2] Something about the term seemed to ring a bell in the social consciousness and "in just a few short decades it rose from relative obscurity to become commonplace."[3]

Late Nineteenth-Century Changes

Three demographic trends would become an integral part of the history of social development in America over the next century: drastic increases in the number and proportion of free blacks, sharp increases in the number and proportion of European

---

1. Wray, *Not Quite White*, 39.
2. Wray, *Not Quite White*, 43.
3. Wray, *Not Quite White*, 41.

immigrants, and a moderate rise in the number and proportion of free whites (non-landholders).[4]

Social observers in the mid to late nineteenth century began to debate both the cause and cure of the phenomenon of white poverty. These observers built their ideas upon a simple idea: "If whiteness bespoke purity and godliness, then poor white trash implied an ungodly, desacralized, polluted whiteness."[5] From that foundation one of the first answers to the problem was to simply declare that, like blacks, the poor white trash were contaminated with impure blood. There was talk of miscegenation. For these members of the Anglo-Saxon race to be demonstrating such deplorable morals, filthy living, and general all-around bad behavior there must be something tainting their blood. Because the problem was biological there was nothing that could be done to change their situation.

By the mid-nineteenth century, the Industrial Revolution was creating new opportunities for economic gain both as entrepreneurs and as general labor in urban locales. In the North there was a mad rush to the cities: "Immigrants, particularly from Ireland, and the continuing ideological influence of Jacksonian impulses marked this period as one of major economic, social, and political instability."[6]

Out of this instability a new class of people began to be formed in both the eastern shores and the Midwest. This new class was neither rich nor poor; they found themselves in the middle of the two extremes. The middle class strove hard to nurture its professionalism, strongly valued group cohesion, order, entrepreneurism, and progress through education, science and technology while at the same time being deeply religious and moralistic.[7]

The middle class saw itself as striving against what it viewed as the excessive and gaudy use of wealth by the rich and the filth and desperate poverty of the poor. It seemed as if this new middle

4. Wray, *Not Quite White*, 45.
5. Wray, *Not Quite White*, 45.
6. Wray, *Not Quite White*, 51.
7. Wray, *Not Quite White*, 52.

Fragmentation of Humanity: Part 2

class was obsessed with cleanliness and urban living in large part because they wanted to distinguish themselves from the poor white trash who were known to be filthy rural dwellers. It was during this time period that those who lived in rural areas began to be seen as "backward and regressive, pre-modern and therefore unenlightened."[8]

The South was for the most part bypassed by the industrial age and remained largely a farming-oriented region. The middle class were nearly non-existent there and as a result, preceding the Civil War, not only were they condemned for being slave holders, but they were also looked upon as being backward and unenlightened.

Matt Wray notes that "out of 12 million people in the Southern US in the 1840s, 4 million were classified as black and 8 million as white. Of the whites, less than 50,000 were slave owners with 20 or more slaves; more than 75 percent of whites owned no slaves at all."[9] The underlying meaning of this, given that fifty thousand people own probably 75 percent or more of the farmable land, was that there were millions of people that fell into the category of poor white trash below the Mason Dixon line.

From a Southern point of view, after the 1896 *Plessey v. Ferguson* ruling which gave judicial support to segregation, there was no black problem—there was a poor white trash problem. Here was this large group of white people that was seen as racially degenerate and distinct from all other whites. Concern was growing that these degenerates would somehow spread the disease of pauperism and filth in some kind of upwardly mobile plague. The result was that "over the course of the latter half of the nineteenth-century, the analytical object of scientized prejudice shifted from people of color—primarily blacks and Indians—to poor white American, foreigners, and immigrants."[10]

Until the end of reconstruction in the 1870s this problem was primarily a Southern problem. However, it was not long before the social and cultural mix of America began to change dramatically.

8. Wray, *Not Quite White*, 52.
9. Wray, *Not Quite White*, 52.
10. Wray, *Not Quite White*, 94.

At the end of the nineteenth and beginning of the twentieth century the Spanish-American war was brought to an end, resulting in large quantities of Mexicans being annexed into America. The conquest of the Philippines opened the door for Filipino immigration; national expansion to the West coast brought encounters with Chinese immigrants. These new transplants were easily classified as non-white. However, during this same time there were nearly twenty-five million immigrants flooding America from the southern and eastern parts of Europe. These people were not the so-called native stock of America, they were not of pure Anglo-Saxon blood. They were a darker shade of pale which meant they were looked upon with suspicion and yet could not be easily classified as non-white.

In 1909, professor Elwood Cubberly wrote,

> About 1882, the character of our immigration changed in a very remarkable manner. Immigration from the north of Europe dropped off rather abruptly and in its place immigration from the south and east of Europe set in and soon developed into a great stream . . . these southern and eastern Europeans are a very different type from the north European who preceded them. Illiterate, docile, lacking in self-reliance and initiative and not possessing Anglo-Teutonic conceptions of law, order, and government, their coming has served to dilute tremendously our national stock, and to corrupt our civic life.[11]

Eugenics

As the presumed biblical support for racial inequality began to lose value, science was already laying the groundwork to save the human race from impurity. "During the years 1863–1868 [Herbert Spencer, Gregor Mendel and Charles Darwin] would all develop aspects of science that began to reveal 'identifiable hereditary units' within cells."[12] In discerning the concept of hereditary traits

---

11. Roediger, *Working Toward Whiteness*, 19.
12. Black, *War against the Weak*, 13.

Fragmentation of Humanity: Part 2

in plants and animals these scientists were simply identifying an aspect of the laws of creation: Traits of one generation of life are passed on to the next generation in plants, animals, and humans.

This new understanding of traits being passed on through biology came into a world full of presuppositions about how things worked. One of those presuppositions, as noted earlier, was that the Anglo-Saxon race was understood to be the pure race from which all other races had diverged or degenerated. The biology of traits and heredity were soon harnessed to the cause of purifying the human race. Another presupposition was the great chain of being, which was slowly being secularized. From that presupposition evolved the notion of missing links. Both blacks and dark whites[13] increasingly began to be identified as potentially subhuman.

These ideas were taking hold of science at the same time as millions of immigrants from all over the world were flooding the United States. It would be an oversimplification to identify the situation that resulted once those immigrants arrived on new shores as a melting pot. The huddled masses came to the land of dreams in ethnic and national huddles, and they moved into neighborhoods of similar huddles. There was very little mixing or melting.

Among the "real" Americans, there was concern that the country was committing "racial suicide" by keeping its borders open. Sociologist E. A. Ross warned of this when he wrote: "The beaten members of beaten breeds from Crotia, Sicily and Armenia flooding through Ellis Island lacked the ancestral foundations of American character, and even if they catch step with us, they and their children will nevertheless impede our progress."[14]

The concept of hereditary traits soon left the realm of the physical and began to find a home in the realm of character, class, and economic status. By the end of the nineteenth century:

> Many leading social progressives devoted to charity and reform now saw crime and poverty as inherited defects that need to be halted for society's sake. When this idea

---

13 The term "dark whites" is documented in Roediger, *Working Toward Whiteness*, 11, 24, 49, 163.

14. Black, *War against the Weak*, 23.

was combined with widespread racism, class prejudice and ethnic hatred that already existed . . . and was juxtaposed with the economic costs to society. . .it created fertile reception for the infant field of eugenics.[15]

By 1903 the fight against the decrease of the German, Nordic, Anglo Saxon population had begun in full force. We must understand that the concept of white supremacy is not simply conceived of as whites against blacks. "Pure white" is a very restrictive and selective color—heredity is all-important. It is not insignificant that the first director of the Station for Experimental Evolution of the Carnegie Institution, based in Cold Springs Harbour, New York, Charles Davenport, began his research by beginning a relationship with the American Breeders Association. The eugenics movement in America was all about restoring the purity of the original breed of human being.

These early theories, however, were only the first stage of development. They were developed into practical outworkings of the law and thus Jim Crow was brought to life. Legal and enforced segregation became the law of the land. An entire system of laws was created to exclude blacks and dark whites from full access to all aspects of Southern American culture and though the laws were not on the books in the North, they were often implemented by public consent.

Darwin's theory of evolution provided the secular framework to naturalize the social order. Social Darwinists began to view society as a conflict for the survival of the fittest. Which link in the great chain of being would find themselves above the other? They combined various evolutionary theories of the time to try to "rationalize and legitimize social inequalities and hierarchies of domination."[16]

There was, however, a problem. Urbanization was emptying the countryside and bringing the less desirables to the cities in droves. That, coupled with the increasing numbers of immigrants of less desirable southern and eastern European origins, led to the

15. Black, *War Against the Weak*, 25.
16. Wray, *Not Quite White*, 69.

Fragmentation of Humanity: Part 2

cities becoming a cesspool of growing crime, disease, immorality, and undesirable human beings. Those who were deemed superior in the eyes of the Social Darwinists seemed to be decreasing. It was as if in the struggle for survival of the fittest, the fittest were on the verge of committing racial suicide.

The Social Darwinist Alfred Russell Wallace reported in 1890,

> In one of my last conversations with Darwin he expressed himself very gloomily on the future of humanity, on the ground that in our modern civilization natural selection had no play, and the fittest did not survive. Those who succeed in the race for wealth are by no means the best or the most intelligent, and it is notorious that our population is more largely renewed in each generation from the lower than from the middle and upper classes.[17]

It seemed that if the fittest were to survive in the eyes of the Social Darwinists it would have to be through unnatural selection. The unfit were seen as subhuman and not worthy to be a part of the natural selection process. They were diseased with a genetic infection. Like any infection the source needed to be "quarantined and then eliminated. Their method of choice was selective breeding—spaying and cutting away the undesirable, while carefully mating and grooming prized stock."[18]

The first woman presidential candidate, Victoria Woodhull, in her book, *The Rapid Multiplication of the Unfit*, wrote in 1891: "The best minds today have accepted the fact that if superior people are desired, they must be bred; and if imbeciles, criminals, paupers and otherwise unfit are undesirable citizens they must not be bred."[19] In keeping with this line of thinking, I.Q. tests were developed to help determine fit from unfit especially when it came to immigration. The search was on to find the feebleminded.

Over the course of time, backed with money from the Carnegie Institute, the eugenics movement beginning in 1903 worked for over a decade to reach their goals. Then in 1914 there came a

---

17. Kevles, *Name of Eugenics*, 70.
18. Black, *War Against the Weak*, 21.
19. Kelves, *Name of Eugenics*, 85.

drastic increase in nationalist fervor brought on by World War I which then gave the momentum to influence the legislative powers to pass the 1924 Immigration Act, which established national quotas and ushered in a long era of immigration restriction.

By 1924 there was such fervent racism that the 1924 Virginia Racial Integrity Acts were put into law. They were a broad set of laws that forbade interracial marriage. These laws not only forbade blacks but also the new immigrant dark whites from marrying white Anglo-Saxon "native" Americans. Within these newly instituted laws were also provisions to enact involuntary sterilization laws that targeted feebleminded whites.

In the fall of 1924, the Virginia State Colony for Epileptics and Feebleminded ordered the sterilization of a young white woman named, Carrie Buck. Her guardian objected and by 1927 the case was heard by the United States Supreme Court. The court upheld the forced sterilization law. In expressing the Court's opinion on the case, Justice Oliver Wendell Holmes wrote,

> It is better for all the world, if instead of waiting to execute degenerate offspring for crime, or to let them starve for their imbecility, society can prevent those who are manifestly unfit from continuing their kind. The principle that sustains compulsory vaccination is broad enough to cover cutting Fallopian tubes. Three generations of imbeciles are enough.[20]

By this time, thirty-three states had enacted involuntary sterilization laws. "By the mid-thirties some twenty thousand sterilizations had been legally performed in the United States."[21] The total number of compulsory sterilizations performed under the guidance of this law was more than sixty thousand.[22]

While the eugenics movement (with regard to whites) was a relative success in Northern States where immigration of dark whites was occurring, the states of the deep south rejected the use of compulsory sterilization on their "poor white trash" population

20. Buck v. Bell (1927). 374 U.S. 200, 47 S. Ct. 584.
21. Kelves, *Name of Eugenics*, 112.
22. http://www.uvm.edu/~lkaelber/eugenics/

(which was the majority of that population and was Anglo-Saxon in origin). Instead of focusing on biological determinism they focused on environmental factors. In the South physical hygiene replaced social hygiene, at least with regard to whites.

Hookworm

The poor white trash problem in the South went against the flow of race and degeneracy ideas that were espoused by the eugenicists. They asked the question: "What was happening in the lives of these Southern Anglo Saxons that caused them to be lazy, apathetic, feeble minded and deformed with a skin that was tallow colored?"[23] The leaders in the South focused their attention on finding a medical solution; surely this condition was caused by some type of chronic disease. If this disease could be determined and cured the afflicted could be "rehabilitated as productive laborers and citizens granting health and prosperity to their local communities and the South and the nation as a whole."[24]

A thorough investigation found that the culprit was not technically a disease nor was it defective germ plasm espoused by the eugenicists but an animal: the hookworm. Further research determined that there was widespread presence of infestation in humans throughout the South (perhaps as high as 40 percent).[25] While it was the Carnegie Institute that funded much of the work of the eugenicists, it was the Rockefeller Foundation that funded the war against the hookworm under the name of the Rockefeller Sanitary Commission to Eradicate Hookworm Disease (RSC).[26]

A crusade was soon underway to eradicate hookworm in the South and not only the dreaded worm but also filth in general. With a moral vigor the reforming army of medics, nurses, and

---

23. Wray, *Not Quite White*, 40.
24. Wray, *Not Quite White*, 96–97.
25. Ettling, *Germ of Laziness*, 2.
26. Ettling, *Germ of Laziness*, 97.

public relations men began the battle of "cleanliness is next to godliness." Matt Wray writes,

> The hookworm campaigners themselves were partial to viewing their work as redemptive, as were most of the era's public health professionals. In their evangelical zeal, crusaders relied upon a message of the essential morality of cleanliness, a message that was especially effective in stirring up religious sentiment and that meshed well with evolutionary models of human perfectibility that were prevalent in the sciences.[27]

Given that this was taking place in the midst of the segregated Jim Crow South the RSC did its best to frame the spread of the disease from the point of view of human contagion that was spread through a specific hierarchy, up the great chain of being: from blacks to poor whites to middle class to upper class. When Charles Stiles demonstrated that hookworms were spread by flies the RSC's Board of Directors suppressed the release of the report considering "the scientific facts to be too scandalous and concluded the letter would hurt rather than help the campaign."[28]

Re-Creating Humans

The basic idea of the degeneration of the human race, whether biological, as with the eugenicists, or environmental, as with the RSC and the hookworm campaign, laid a foundation for a new kind of human being, one that was seen as evermore perfectible. The goal was the perfection of a superior race of human beings. The universal understanding of those that espoused such notions was that the superior race would be the Anglo-Saxon or Aryan race.

Popular ideas spread quickly; the study of eugenics was developing not only in America but simultaneously in England and Germany, as well as other places. In 1934 Dr. Joseph S. DeJohnette, long a powerful voice in Virginia eugenics and a major influence

---

27. Ettling, *Germ of Laziness*, 110.
28. Ettling, *Germ of Laziness*, 124.

Fragmentation of Humanity: Part 2

in its sterilization program "urged the legislature to broaden the sterilization law . . . [because] the Germans are beating us at our own game."[29]

However, by this time the eugenics movement in the United States was becoming suspect. In 1935, Herman J. Juller, an American geneticist was noting that it had become "hopelessly perverted."[30] By the summer of 1944 news of just how successful the German eugenics program had become began to trickle into the United States as reports of the devastation found in the concentration camps was heard for the first time. The number of victims continued to climb with each new report and by the time the war was over nearly six million Jews were dead, not to mention Christians. The ideas of the impurity of the blood in the Jewish people that began our study of racism came to full fruition at the hands of the Nazi regime.

> The resulting shock and mortification did more to discredit racism—at least in its blatant ideological forms—than had any previous historical event."[31] The eugenics movement and the concept of physically manipulating the lives of individuals by government mandate with an eye toward race purity were discredited in the public eye. Within the United States, there was a growing realization among those concerned with international relations that Jim Crow not only was analogous to Nazi treatment of the Jews and thus morally indefensible but was also contrary to the national interest.[32]

The Slow Train of Change

That being the case, it would be another twenty years before the Jim Crow laws were outlawed. Ideas that have been engrained in the hearts and minds of a people for hundreds of years do not change

29. Kevles, *Name of Eugenics,* 116
30. Kelves, *Name of Eugenics,* 116.
31. Fredrickson, *Racism: A Short History,* 128.
32. Fredrickson, *Racism: A Short History,* 129.

with the end of a war or the passage of a law. In the South Jim Crow was the written law of the land but in the North, it was the unwritten law of the land. Some ten years after the end of World War II, the long-standing Supreme Court decision of 1896, *Plessey v. Ferguson,* which had upheld State laws requiring racial segregation in education for nearly fifty years, was found to be unconstitutional by the Supreme Court ruling *Brown v. Board of Education.*

The new ruling was not well-received in the South as the diatribe of the man from St. Augustine at the beginning of this chapter demonstrated. Racial tensions were at an all-time high. America was anything but united on this issue, especially in the South. And then this music came on the scene that took the hillbilly music of poor white trash and mixed it with the race music of blacks and unintentionally/intentionally blurred the lines of segregation and united the subhumans against the humans. One could turn on the radio and supposedly hear a blues singer sing the song "All Shook Up" only to find out later that the singer was white. Conversely, one could hear a hillbilly song called "Maybelline" on the radio and really enjoy it, until it was revealed that the singer was black.

This new music was desegregating the culture because the music itself was color blind. The Jim Crow view of the world that had held sway for nearly fifty years in the South saw blacks and whites trying to intermingle—saw subhuman blacks and subhuman poor white trash creating a new music. It was only logical that the resulting music by necessity had to be degenerate; subhumans cannot produce good music. They are nothing but savages, brute beasts trying to bring the Anglo-Saxon race down to their level. Etched in the collective memory of the 1950s south are associations of the degenerates as lazy, dirty, and immoral. The result was that this new music must by default share those qualities. Rock and roll was an affront to the status quo of the "native" and "pure" American Anglo-Saxon race. The courts might force integration but there was no way in the world music was going to corrupt their children. The battle was on.

9

Fragmentation in Summary

THE VERY BRIEF HISTORY, given above, of the unfolding of philosophy in the modern age is the story of the building of the bomb that shook the modern world into the postmodern world. For the survivors who understand the damage of the intellectual and societal blast which occurred, all that is left is fragmentation.

This conflict over music was deeper than it seemed. It was a clash between two radically different views of the world. The modern world was trying to keep the postmodern world from tearing down its kingdom. However, it is doubtful that those who were in the midst of the struggle knew the depth of the struggle. One side was afraid of losing what they had worked so hard to produce. The other side was afraid of being trapped in an artificial world that pretended there was meaning when there was not.

The modern point of view was the first to impact the world in a noticeable way. The concept of modernity refers to a particular era in human history that is characterized by scientific thought rather than metaphysical or supernatural belief. It was generated around the end of the eighteenth century into the turn of the nineteenth century. Perhaps it began to flourish in the blood of the American Revolution.

Louder Than Words

Those who embraced salvation in independence and innovation mistakenly thought that the world was an unblemished whole. However, that wholeness would have been questioned daily by those who carried the weight of the Industrial Revolution on their backs working fourteen-hour days for pennies; their only respite to go home to the stinking slums, too cold in the winter, too hot in the summer. The whole family trudging home from a long day at work—if they made it through the day alive or without being dismembered. Never mind the slaves, the Native Americans, and the immigrants that did not fit the profile of what it meant to be an American.

The roots of modernism that began growing were not rooted in biblical Christianity, as some suppose, but in a completely transformed thinking about the Scripture that had never existed before. As modernity focused on the individual and industry those concepts somehow began to be equated with the advancement of the kingdom of God, especially in America. It is doubtful that Jesus would have recognized this revolution as a part of his kingdom, but such was the theory of those with money and power and a nagging conscience.

Postmodernity on the other hand could be said to have been birthed in the French Revolution. It is a cry against the modern age because it sees the absence of wholeness in life everywhere. There is no foundation upon which to build because the forms are nothing but mathematical equations irrelevant to the material world—a random swerve being the source of all that is.

Signs of the Times

Two years after America became a nation the Swiss artist Henri Fuseli understood that the foundation of modernity was shaky, if not already starting to crumble. Noting his work "The Artist Overwhelmed by the Grandeur of Ancient Ruins" William Tronzo writes,

Fragmentation in Summary

> The Fuseli is a depressing image. The body of the artist (or his surrogate) flaccid with grief, signals an end to the age-old debate between the ancients and moderns. This is an image of a culture on the downward slide, where the capacity for renewal seems to be on the verge of slipping away forever.[1]

By the beginning of the nineteenth century the wholeness of creation, in those with eyes to see, was gone. Science with its heavenly forms of mathematical precision had, by faith, destroyed the foundation of creation. In other words, from the time of Nicholas Cusanus (1401–64) to the nineteenth century, the foundations of science and philosophy, including a basis for believing in reality, were all destroyed, from a humanist viewpoint.

Rethinking

Please do not misunderstand, people still believed the Bible as a sourcebook and guide. They believed in progress. They believed in science. However, they had long since transformed the contents of these things into something that would no longer be recognized by the Creator, with regard to the original intent of the world and the revelation of the word of God.

The words were the same, but the meaning applied to them had been torn to shreds and scattered to the wind. Creation was no longer whole. It was fragmented—not from God's point of view but from the human perspective. How could that be? The simple explanation is that humanity rebelled against its Creator and the wholeness he produced. Apart from Adam, Eve, and Jesus, no other human being has been able to experience the wholeness of creation.

However, it is important to understand that the creation apart from humanity is still whole. It is the way that God intends it to be. But because of the rebellion of human beings against the Creator the world is cursed in order to make life more difficult for

---

1. Tronzo, *Fragment: An Incomplete History*, 1–2.

rebellious humans. Why? Because more than anything God wants to restore the relationship between himself and any human being that is willing to humble themselves before their maker. The shattering that exists is a call to repentance; a call to see with different eyes.

The Earth is the Lord's and the fullness thereof. The world is not fragmented; however, humans are. Every human on the planet experiences the fragmentation of the rebellion against God. Yet we do not all see with the same eyes. There are at least three sets of eyes with which to view the world. One group, by faith, sees all of existence as broken and fragmented. The second group, by faith, sees the world as whole even though there is no foundation for such a leap of faith in their foundation of science or in their religion. The third group, by faith, looks at the world and sees humanity alone as broken. The world is still cursed (people are still dying, disease is rampant, death is all around) but within that brokenness they see hope in the death and resurrection of Jesus Christ. They look forward to restoration, a restored wholeness for human beings and the end of fragmentation.

Eyes to See

Very few people take the time to notice that the way one lives life reveals a way of viewing the world. I was in my fifties before I became aware of the vision impairment of humans. I was raised to believe that the world was worthless and condemned, worthy of only destruction. I did not know that I had been taught a way to view the world. In my late twenties I began to see the world as whole, restored in Jesus and slowly working out that restoration in every area of life. That point of view was certainly more hopeful, however, in time I began to see that economic progress is not a signifier of how the world is progressing. There have been many empires which have gathered much wealth, but they have fallen, both before and after Christ.

The kingdom is not slowly growing out of the curse and reversing it. The world is not getting better with each passing day.

Fragmentation in Summary

There is a reason for the discontent and even the hopelessness of people that are not able to lift themselves up by their bootstraps into a better position in life. The least of these will be with us until the end of the age—and as long as humans are able to die, the earthly creation is still under the curse.

Certainly, Jesus Christ inaugurated a new age. He sits at the right hand of the Father ruling and reigning in heaven. Yet, Satan still roams about like a roaring lion seeking those he may devour. That crafty lion has been putting on a lot of weight over the two plus millennia since Jesus took the throne. There seems to be no stopping his feeding spree anytime soon. And yet, Jesus does reign in created heaven. The promise of a new age on Earth is unfulfilled yet still true.

These days, I am not foolish enough to think that I can put together the pieces in the correct order so that the finished picture can be seen. Yet I wonder if the two main ways of seeing the Scriptures are not more influenced by economic theory than Scripture. In the nineteenth century those that knew they would never be economically prosperous or be able to pick themselves up by their own bootstraps found hope in the pre-millennial return of Jesus. They needed to escape the world as it was. At the same time, those that were doing well in the new economy began to read Scripture through the lens of a long, slow yet steady, increase in the kingdom of God on Earth topped off by Jesus coming back and saying: "Well, done you good and faithful servants."

I am starting to understand that both views (and I have embraced them both in my lifetime) are too simplistic for the real world, the cursed world. The curse is too entwined in humanity to be eliminated from people who have not died to themselves, and dying to oneself takes a lifetime. Thus, the reason for this section of the book.

My understanding is that we are at a crossroad where humanity is seeing modernity getting closer to the end of the road and post-modernity beginning to blossom. As the stabilizing fiction of modernity comes to an end, the devastation and reality of fragmentation will come into clearer focus. And we will find ourselves in a place that is best described by this well-known poem:

> Humpty Dumpty sat on a wall,
> Humpty Dumpty had a great fall.
> All the king's horses and all the king's men
> Couldn't put Humpty together again.[2]

Postmodernism will then have its reign of terror. But that is not the end of the story because the author of the human race has written a different story and that story is a mystery.

For now:

>   Fragmentation
>   Is all around us
>   Splintering us: The human race
>   (If that construct ever really existed)
>   Into billions of I's that cannot see
>   The whole
>   (Which none of us have ever experienced
>   but is rumored to have existed)
>   Becomes a myth too big to believe
>   And we wonder why the world is divided
>   Into gingham dogs and calico cats
>   Who will soon
>   Litter the face of the earth with their remains
>   Leaving nature to die a slow death
>   Because it cannot take care of itself
>   Despite our constructs that deem otherwise
>   Who'd a thunk
>   That a big bang
>   Could be so destructive?
>   Now if I could only find the right word
>   I mean
>   THE WORD

---

2. Denslow, *Denslow's Humpty Dumpty*, 2.

10

The Spirit Walk

IN THE MIDST OF the chaos that is the twenty-first century, I have hope for the future because of the death and resurrection of Jesus Christ. I have hope for the present because Jesus sent the Holy Spirit to minister in the time between the times. This first became evident to me when I was in my early twenties. I was sitting in my car in a parking lot of Illinois State University. It may very well have been the first day of classes—a new beginning. I was getting ready to go to class, but I was early enough that I had time to pray. And these were the words that came out of my mouth: "Dear God, I don't care how much it costs, do what you've got to do to make me like Jesus. Amen." When I was done, I went on my way. But that prayer would never leave me.

Now some forty years later I am still learning to embrace the work of the Holy Spirit in the midst of this wonderful, and simultaneously, horrible outworking of creation that is unfolding all around us. I am being helped in that process through the writing of H. Evan Runner. For instance, in his work *Scripture, Religion and Political Task* he writes,

> Our following of Christ comes only after the completion of Christ's Mediatorial work and the pouring out of the Holy Spirit: after Calvary, after the resurrection, after

the ascension, after Pentecost. To follow Christ aright we must first be engrafted into Christ by the Holy Spirit, who continues to lead the Church into the Truth.[1]

In the work *Cui Bono* he writes,

> With Abraham we have the same thing. Jehovah spoke with the whole Abraham. And the work of faith by the Holy Spirit, that was a moving-day for the large household of a shepherd-prince. And the promises of God—heavy with spiritual gifts—were no mystical words of "being in communion with God in the loneliness of the soul"—no, but rather that old Abraham would have of Sarah a son of promise, and that in his seed the Earth would be blessed.[2]

Reformational writer Keith Sewell, in his work *The Crisis of Evangelical Christianity*, writes,

> Amid the deficiencies and follies of contemporary Evangelicalism, all Christians would do well to say daily, "I believe in the sovereignty of the Holy Spirit." Renewal is impossible, in that it is beyond the capacity of any or all Christians to achieve. It is beyond all human accomplishment."[3]

I could not agree more with that notion. He continues:

> Paul taught that the church was "founded upon" apostles and prophets—in the way that a building is erected on its foundations, the point being that the building rests upon its foundations but does not consist wholly of its foundations (Eph 2:20–3:5). The entire Pentecostal-charismatic movement persistently flounders before two complementary historical realities: (1) The first century church had apostles and prophets, but no canonical New Testament, and (2) in subsequent centuries the church has a canonical New Testament but is without apostles and prophets. All of which is not to deny that Christians

---

1. Runner, *Walking in the Way*, 2:188.
2. Runner, *Walking in the Way*, 1:115.
3. Sewell, *Crisis of Evangelical Christianity*, loc. 4742–43.

The Spirit Walk

are always called by the Holy Spirit to be both apostolic and prophetic.

The standpoint outlined above is sometimes referred to as cessationism. It has strong support among both patristic and Reformation authors. Nevertheless, it is a regrettably negative and potentially misleading term. A term such as "apostolically-foundational" might be preferable. Asserting that the church was built upon the testimony and teaching of apostles and prophets whose office has now ceased, along with the associated charismata, does not entail that the person and work of the Holy Spirit are denied, or that he has ceased to provide outstanding, gifted men and women to the church of Christ. Neither does it mean that remarkable experiences of healing and restoration are not now occasionally embellishment.[4]

This is a thoughtful response to the modern charismatic movement. I think there is much wrong with both sides of the controversy in the church over the Holy Spirit and his work. I certainly do not have it figured out and I believe that if we think we can figure out what the sovereign Holy Spirit can or cannot do, will or will not do, we have set ourselves up for a fall.

From my perspective the argument for cessationism from Scripture is actually very weak. It gains its strength not directly from Scripture but from an interpretation of Scripture rooted and grounded in what I would call Enlightenment philosophy. The passage that is often used to support the cessation of the gifts of the Spirit is 1 Cor 13:

> If I speak in the tongues of men and of angels, but have not love, I am a noisy gong or a clanging cymbal. And if I have prophetic powers, and understand all mysteries and all knowledge, and if I have all faith, so as to remove mountains, but have not love, I am nothing. If I give away all I have, and if I deliver up my body to be burned, but have not love, I gain nothing. Love is patient and kind; love does not envy or boast; it is not arrogant or rude. It

---

4. Sewell, *Crisis of Evangelical Christianity*, loc. 3670–83.

does not insist on its own way; it is not irritable or resentful; it does not rejoice at wrongdoing but rejoices with the truth. Love bears all things, believes all things, hopes all things, endures all things. Love never ends. As for prophecies, they will pass away; as for tongues, they will cease; as for knowledge, it will pass away. For we know in part and we prophesy in part, but when the perfect comes, the partial will pass away. When I was a child, I spoke like a child, I thought like a child, I reasoned like a child. When I became a man, I gave up childish ways. For now, we see in a mirror dimly, but then face to face. Now I know in part; then I shall know fully, even as I have been fully known. So now faith, hope, and love abide, these three; but the greatest of these is love.

The passage that is crucial for the doctrine of cessation is:

As for prophecies, they will pass away; as for tongues, they will cease; as for knowledge, it will pass away. For we know in part and we prophesy in part, but when the perfect comes, the partial will pass away.

I believe that to be 100 percent true. If perhaps, I was of a different status in life I might believe that the perfect, or the fullness of the age, the maturity of the age, or the age that is lacking nothing necessary to completeness, had actually come. But from my perspective, the completeness, the perfect, is still a long way off.

Many try to say that the written word of God is "the perfect." Therefore, now that we have the completed Bible the perfect has come. Sewell seems to subtly allude to this. The underlying emphasis of that is: We have all we need. Yet, as someone who has struggled his whole life to simply keep his head above water, I find it extremely difficult to believe that the perfect has come.

In fact, if we call the Bible, as we know it, the perfect, I believe that we are bordering on blasphemy because completion of the written word of God did not end the lacking or give us answers to questions; all things have not been put under Christ. From my insignificant place in this world, I understand the perfect to be Jesus Christ who sits on the throne ruling and reigning until

The Spirit Walk

all things are placed under his feet. When "all things" are placed under his authority and the rebellion is put to an end, then and only then, will prophecies and words of knowledge cease because there will be no need for them. Until the least of these are able to know themselves as they are known, there is a need for the gifts and fruits of the Spirit.

That being said, I have no affinity for the actions of those who claim to have the authority of God and then twist it to their own advantage, financial or otherwise. I certainly have no use for the power of positive thinking masquerading as a substitute for faith. All manipulation is ungodly. God will judge both those who deny his power and those who use that power to their own gain.

The other aspect that is often overlooked is that Satan is not yet bound. As Peter tells us: "Be sober-minded; be watchful. Your adversary the devil prowls around like a roaring lion, seeking someone to devour."[5] Paul also tells us that "we do not wrestle against flesh and blood, but against the rulers, against the authorities, against the cosmic powers over this present darkness, against the spiritual forces of evil in the heavenly places."[6]

Our enemies are *not* flesh and blood, neither are they simply wrong ideas: they are spiritual forces of evil in heavenly places. For this reason, spiritual gifts are needed to thwart the deeds of those who are daily trying to take us out of the picture. The world is more complicated than most people want to think about. Evil is a presence from outside the earthly realm. The rationalism that has attempted to debunk the spiritual realm and the necessity of fighting our battles in that realm is one of the greatest ploys of the enemy against the church in the history of the world.

My heart longs for the unreasonable good news to be manifested in the lives of believers. I need the unreasonable to impact my life with a vengeance because my life is still fragmented. Certainly, one could look at my life rationally and say "this is where you messed up. You could have done this differently." That is all fine and dandy, but that does not take into the consideration the

---

5. 1 Pet 5:8.
6. Eph 6:12.

fragmentation of the fall. The reality is that, given the mess that was my life, I could not do things differently. I did not have the will or the power to do anything other than what I did.

The written word of God did nothing to heal my brokenness. The church, as it is, could do nothing to heal my brokenness. I needed more than words, more than ideas to bring healing to my damaged life. I needed the good news that Jesus can heal the blind, raise the dead, turn water into wine. In other words, I needed to experience the fact that God can heal my brokenness now.

The Holy Spirit working through Jesus two thousand years ago does me no good. Those who are fragmented like me need to know that Jesus is willing and able to bring restoration here, now, in the time after the New Testament. I want him to do what he said he would do, the same things that he did when he was walking the Earth. Humanity is not less broken in the twenty-first century than it was in the first. I will not need to be restored in the sweet by and by; I need it now. If the full outworking of the good news is not meant for anyone except the ones who can afford to purchase it, then pass the Kool-Aid so I can get to a place where the words of the gospel are meant to be taken seriously.

Do not get me wrong; I understand the impact of a truly Christian philosophy promoted by the Reformational branch of the church. It is essential for a right understanding of how the world works. However, a right understanding of how the world works does not heal the broken-hearted. The Reformational followers, just like their Reformed precursors, have done a decent job of digging deep into the Scriptures. Yet, the end result is not harmony and oneness but dissention and quibbling over the meanings of words.

Hour after hour, book after book, sermon after sermon is spent haggling over words. For the Reformed branch it is the word of the Scriptures while for the Reformational branch it is words of philosophy. Certainly, there is some wonderful work going on but to the making of books there is no end. Do we really need a more detailed understanding of time or of the book of Romans? What we need is to use our time to do the good news. We need to be the living word of God to the broken and desperate. We need to be the power of God in the midst of a powerless world. The salvation that is offered from modern, traditional Christian points of view in our day and age is nothing more than a babbling of words. What is truly needed is the power of God displayed in broken people's lives through restoration.

This is where I find myself at this point in the process. I have uncovered the knowledge that I am fractured but healing. Yet, the end result of gathering all this information was the opening of my eyes to see not just my own fragmentation but that of all the western world and its people. It also let me see the fragmentation of the church, each one doing what is right in their own eyes, trusting in their own strength. That, in turn, produces the resulting irrelevance of the church. In other words, we seem impotent to do the very thing that the work of Jesus is supposed to do: destroy the works of the evil one.

11

Pressing On

THE WRITING OF RUNNER reminded me of the times when God had overwhelmed me with his presence. I began to understand that what I needed in my life was the whole word of God applied in time and space. I needed the words, and I needed the gifts of the spirit. I needed to work out my salvation with fear and trembling and I also needed the fruits of the Spirit. I needed to be a whole human being. To become that, I needed both the Word and the Spirit.

I found myself occasionally saying such things in pastor meetings and other events. Sometimes it would spark joy in people's eyes. They got it. They knew they needed it. Other times it sparked indifference or disdain. Some had been burned by the foolishness of many in the charismatic circles. Some had been raised to believe it was all of the devil. I simply pressed on to see where it would lead. Would God eventually show up and actually do something that could only come from him, or would I learn to not believe the word of God and replace it with my theology and philosophy?

My thinking was drawn to the ministry of John Wimber, from which the Vineyard Christian Fellowships emerged. By this time, he had already been dead for nearly twenty years. I bought all his books and many of the books that were in the bibliographies of his books.

Pressing On

Now, I did not just accept everything carte blanche, I tried to be wise. The thing that I loved about John Wimber was his openness and honesty. The following is a summary of what I learned from reading his books, watching his videos and being ministered to by Blain Cook; one of his his coworkers in the eighties and nineties:

> I can't do anything for anyone. All I do is pray. . . . If something happens it didn't come from me. If anyone ever tells you that they are the ones doing the gifts turn and run in the opposite direction as fast as you can. . . . The gifts of the spirit are from God to God and all for his glory, with the goal of advancing the Kingdom of God through Jesus Christ.

Reading is one thing; actually doing the stuff, as Wimber used to say, is on a whole other level. In my own life, I have been able to receive from the Spirit of God fairly successfully, leading to healing of many past hurts. But when it comes to passing that along there is still a bit of a disconnect. I pray for people from time to time in a style that Wimber might call a soaking prayer. I simply lay hands on people and start to pray, usually in tongues for the simple fact that I do not have a clue what people need, nor do I know what God wants to do. I do not get words of knowledge or wisdom very often. Sometimes when I think I have one it seems to fall flat and do nothing. That is not because God is not doing something, more often than not, it is because I am still in kindergarten in the things of the Spirit. The reason for that is I have not found a safe place in the church to work these things out with honest fear and trembling.

I have a few friends that I pray with and for, at times, for an extended period, say forty-five minutes to an hour, sometimes longer. Things happen. The people being prayed for know that something is going on in their bodies, but rarely is it clear exactly what God is doing. We have yet to be able to translate the nonverbal experiences into words.

Perhaps part of the problem is that the church today wants a safe God. However, as Mr. Beaver said when asked if Aslan the great lion was safe . . . "Safe? Don't you hear what Mrs. Beaver tells you? Who said anything about safe? 'Course he isn't safe. But he's good. He's the King, I tell you."[1] A safe God can't save you from yourself. But then again, in my experience, most people who follow Christ do not want to be saved from themselves, they simply want to escape life—the very thing that we have been called to.

In the course of this time of seeking the restoration that salvation promises, something changed inside me. I was convicted of sin that I had been harboring for years. Nothing had happened in my everyday life to bring that to my attention. In my head, up to that point, I had done nothing wrong. Yet, those times that the spirit moved on me seemed to open a door that allowed me to see my sin and then to overcome my fears, confess and receive forgiveness. God had removed a huge spiritual burden manifested by sin that I had unconsciously been carrying around for years. Until that time, I thought I was in the right. Afterwards I understood that I was in sin and needed to repent. No one spoke to me about it at all. It was completely the work of the Holy Spirit.

Slowly I began to understand what true grace and love were meant to be: tools that allow the Holy Spirit to produce his fruits in our lives. It is not our job to produce the fruits of the Spirit: love, joy, peace, patience, kindness, goodness, faithfulness, gentleness, self-control. It is our job to walk in the grace and love of God abiding in the vine Jesus so that God the Holy Spirit can flow from Jesus into us producing fruit. It means the death of the Dewey Gospel, the gospel of "pull yourself up by your bootstraps." The gospel of teaching people to be better people. Being conformed to the image of Christ is impossible without the fruit of the Holy Spirit.

I realize that when it comes to working out this salvation with fear and trembling, I am still in kindergarten at the age of sixty. I continue to pursue these things because I understand the depth of fragmentation in every area of life. Yet, I am constantly reminded of the restoration that Jesus provided physically, emotionally, spiritually, and even economically to people whom he encountered. He did not give them money, he did not give them advice, he gave

---

1. Lewis, *Lion, the Witch and the Wardrobe*, 59.

Pressing On

them nothing at all, but the Holy Spirit through him gave them life in its fullness as they were able to receive it. Some to whom he ministered went home sad because they refused to do as he asked. Some received a great physical restoration and ignored giving thanks to God. Some received with great joy and gave thanks to God.

12

Realizing I Am Not Alone

IN 2018, N. T. Wright released his biography of Paul the apostle. Up to that time, I had not been a huge fan. Some years earlier I had tried to read his book *Evil and the Justice of God*. At the time, I was very much into R. J. Rushdoony and law was very dear to my heart. Thus, I could not hear what Wright was saying. Closer to the truth is that I did not want to hear what he was saying. With that background, I cannot really tell you what drew me to the new book—it must have been that it was a biography and not theologically oriented.

When I finally started reading it, I could not put it down. Wright's thought processes seemed to click with me. When I finished, I started a collection of his early writings entitled *Pauline Perspectives*. After that I worked my way chronologically through five volumes stopping about halfway through *Paul and the Faithfulness of God*. I ended up getting sidetracked by something else for a while.

It was in *Paul and the Faithfulness of God* that Wright first mentioned Reformational authors—with a footnote to a book by Richard Middleton and Brian J. Walsh: *Truth Is Stranger Than It Used to Be*. In the second volume of *Paul and the Faithfulness of God*, Wright notes Nicolas Wolterstorff, as well as Walsh and S.

C. Kreesmaat who co-wrote *Colossians Remixed* and Middleton's book, *A New Heaven and a New Earth*.

I read a lot of N. T. Wright in a short amount of time and it began to grow on me. It gave my eyes new lenses so that I could see in a broader frame of reference both the Reformed and Reformational points of view. The fragmented parts of my thinking seemed to be coming together as a whole with regard to theology. And then, as I was researching N. T. Wright, I came upon a Youtube video of his show "Ask NT Wright Anything." The topic was cessationism and the following is an abbreviated text version of what he had to say:

> I think the biblical argument for cessation goes back to 1 Cor 13 where Paul says "Whether there be tongues they shall cease." But he doesn't actually say when and it looks as though in that passage, in 1 Cor 13, he's actually talking about the ultimate future. And that in the present there are all sorts of gifts which won't be necessary in the future. He contrasts that with Love which will be all the more important in God's new creation. You know we won't stop loving in God's new creation but there will be all sorts of things that we won't need to do anymore and speaking in tongues will be one of them.
>
> I remember sharing this (nervousness about a new stage of life) with a cousin of mine who was in a quiet way a charismatic Christian in Canada. And she said, "Well, it may well be that God will give you something like the gift of tongues." And she prayed for me and the next thing I knew I was praying in tongues . . . Very startled . . . this wasn't supposed to happen. I hadn't known when I was going to stay with this cousin that any such thing was on the agenda at all.
>
> But she was absolutely right that there were many, many times . . . that was 1986 over thirty years ago . . . when I have needed to pray into a particular situation but have had actually no idea of a specific thing I ought to be praying for.
>
> Now Paul says something like that in Rom 8: We don't know what to pray for, but the Spirit prays within

us. I'm not sure whether in Rom 8 he's talking about praying in tongues though some people have said that...

But be that as it may I have found on many occasions that the use of tongues in private prayer [I have never exercised this gift in public and have no particular desire to] has enabled me to hold people in situations within the love of God in a way which for some reason seems to be different from saying: "I prayed for so and so" And I'm just content with that.[1]

It took me a while to process those words. Here was a biblical scholar extraordinaire who was not ashamed to say that he spoke in tongues. What blew me away even more is that his experience was unexpectedly, remarkably like my own. Maybe I was not a freak after all. Maybe it truly was God that was tearing me down and building me back up upon a stronger foundation over and over and over. And maybe, just maybe, he was going to continue to do so until the day of Christ Jesus.

I was reminded of Ezek 12:2: "Son of man, you dwell in the midst of a rebellious house, which has eyes to see but does not see, and ears to hear but does not hear; for they are a rebellious house." Which then reminded me of the words of Jesus in Matt 13:13–15:

> This is why I speak to them in parables, because seeing they do not see, and hearing they do not hear, nor do they understand. Indeed, in their case the prophecy of Isaiah is fulfilled that says: "You will indeed hear but never understand, and you will indeed see but never perceive. For this people's heart has grown dull, and with their ears they can barely hear, and their eyes they have closed, lest they should see with their eyes and hear with their ears and understand with their heart and turn, and I would heal them."

From there, I began to think about my first encounter with N. T. Wright's work. And it then dawned on me that when I was first introduced to N. T. Wright, I could not see what he was saying because I had eyes, but I could not see. I was blind to what he was

---

1. Wright, "Cessationism and Why I Pray in Tongues," 7:29.

saying about the Word of God. Could my theology have caused me to be blind to the truth? With a bit of fear and trepidation, I decided to put that theory to the test. I bought a copy of the *Evil and the Justice of God* and started to read.

I read it in just a couple of days, and I really enjoyed it. I understood it. I embraced it. Why? Because God had changed my heart. He had removed my dullness; he opened my eyes so that I could hear what God was saying through N. T. Wright's words.

The point in all of this, at least for me, is that God seems to be giving me eyes to see things that I never wanted to see. I thought I already had twenty-twenty vision regarding the things of God but what I realized was that I had selective blindness. I was picking and choosing what I would allow God to say to me. If it did not fit with my view of the world (even if that view was not God's view of the world) I did not want anything to do with it because I had this deep inner desire, no wait, perhaps it was a desperate need, to see myself and my ideas as right. To be found in error would bring my kingdom tumbling down and that, I feared, would be the death of me.

And yet, here I am standing in the rubble of the truths I used to hold dear, with a thankful heart. God is still answering the prayer I prayed when I was nineteen: do what you've got to do to make me like you. And he is doing this despite the personal cost to me, in spite of the pain that it brings. Why? Because he loves me enough to correct my course so that I will arrive at the destination he has planned for me in this age, during my life on this planet. He has been waiting on me to be ready for nearly sixty years. Yet, while he was waiting, he was also healing me from the inside out to facilitate my readiness.

I find myself grateful that God is not like me because if he were, he would have already sided with the Queen of Hearts and said, "Off with his head!" Thankfully, the writer of Lamentations has given us these wonderful words:

> This I call to mind, and therefore I have hope: The steadfast love of the Lord never ceases; his mercies never come to an end; they are new every morning; great is

your faithfulness. "The Lord is my portion," says my soul, "therefore I will hope in him."[2]

As for me, O Lord, judge my cause . . . and find the blood of Jesus as payment.

---

2. Lam 21–24.

Bibliography

Aristotle. *The Complete Aristotle*. Trans. Steve Thomas. Ebooks@Adelaide, 2007. Kindle.
Axelrod, David. "The History of Rock and Roll." Time-Life Television, 1995.
Barnes, Gilbert H. *The Anti-Slavery Impulse: 1830–1844*. New York: Harbinger, 1964.
Barrett, William. *Death of the Soul: From Descartes to the Computer*. Garden City, NY: Anchor, 1987.
———. *Irrational Man*. Garden City, NY: Anchor, 1962.
Black, Edwin. *War against the Weak: Eugenics and America's Campaign to Create a Master Race*. Dialog, 2003.
Cassirer, Ernst. *The Individual and the Cosmos in Renaissance Philosophy*. New York: Harper Torch, 1963.
Comte, Auguste. *A General View of Positivism*. Cambridge: Cambridge University Press, 2009.
Davis, David Brion. *Inhuman Bondage: The Rise and Fall of Slavery in the New World*. Oxford: Oxford University Press, 2006.
Denslow, W. W. *Denslow's Humpty Dumpty*. New York: G.W. Dillingham, 1903.
Dewey, John. *John Dewey Premium Collection*. e-art now, 2016.
———. *The Problems of Men*. New York: Philosophical Library, 1946. Kindle.
Dickens, Charles. *A Tale of Two Cities*. E-BooksDirectory.com., 2007.
Diltz, James. *The Great Road: The Building of the Baltimore and Ohio, the Nation's First Railroad, 1828–1853*. Palo Alto, CA: Stanford University Press, 1993.
Dooyeweerd, Herman. *A New Critique of Theoretical Thought, vol. 1*. Grand Rapids: Paideia, 1984.
———. *Reformation and Scholasticism in Philosophy, vol. 2*. Translated by Ray Togtmann, edited by Daniel Strauss. Grand Rapids: Paideia, 2012.
———. *Roots of Western Culture: Pagan, Secular, and Christian Options*. Grand Rapids: Paideia, 2012.
Dunlevy, James A. "Economic Opportunity and the Responses of 'Old' and 'New' Migrants to the United States." *The Journal of Economic History* 38:4 (1978) 75–92.

Bibliography

Dwight, Sereno E. *The Biography of Jonathan Edwards*. London: Ball, Arnold, and Col, 1840. Reprinted by Christianebooks.com, 2015. Kindle.

Eby, Fredrick, and Charles Flinn Arrowood. *The Development of Modern Education*. New York: Prentice Hall, 1934.

Edwards, Jonathan. *Justification by Faith Alone*. 2016. Kindle.

Estep, William R. *The Anabaptist Story*. Grand Rapids: Eerdmans, 1996.

Ettling, John. *The Germ of Laziness: Rockefeller Philanthropy and Public Health in the New South*. Cambridge, MA: Harvard University Press, 1981.

Fredrickson, George M. *The Black Image in the White Mind: The Debate on Afro-American Character and Destiny*. Middletown, CT: Wesleyan University Press, 1987.

———. *The Inner Civil War: Northern Intellectuals and the Crisis of the Union*. Chicago: University of Illinois Press, 1993.

———. *Racism: A Short History*. Princeton: Princeton University Press, 2002.

Gardiner, Patrick. *Kierkegaard: A Very Short Introduction*. Oxford: Oxford University Press, 1988.

Gassendi, Pierre. *The Selected Works of Pierre Gassendi*. Translated by Craig Brush. New York: Johnson, 1972.

Gaukroger, Stephen. *The Collapse of Mechanism and the Rise of Sensibility*. Oxford: Oxford University Press, 2010.

———. *The Emergence of Scientific Culture: Science and the Shaping of Modernity, 1210–1685*. Oxford: Oxford University Press, 2006.

Gilbert, Martin. *The First World War: A Complete History*. New York: Rosetta, 2014. Kindle.

———. *The Second World War: A Complete History*. New York: Rosetta, 2014. Kindle.

"The Great Chain of Being."*Encyclopedia Britannica*. https//:www.britannica.com/topic/great-chain-of-being. Online.

Green, J. A. *Life and Work of Pestalozzi*. London: University of London Press, 1913.

Hall, G. Stanley. *Life and Confessions of a Psychologist*. London: D. Appleton, 1923.

Hammond, Phillip E. *Religion and Personal Autonomy: The Third Disestablishment in America*. Columbia, SC: University of South Carolina Press, 1992.

Hawthorne, Nathaniel. *Selected Letters of Nathaniel Hawthorne*. Edited by Joel Myerson. Columbus, OH: Ohio State University Press, 2002.

Hillstrom, Kevin, and Laurie Collier Hillstrom. *The Industrial Revolution in America: Agriculture and Meatpacking*. Vol 8. Santa Barbara, CA: ABC-CLIO, 2007.

———. *The Industrial Revolution in America: Overview/Comparison*. Vol. 9, edited by Kevin Hillstrom. Santa Barbara: ABC-CLIO, 2007.

———. *The Industrial Revolution in America: Railroads*. Vol. 2, edited by Kevin Hillstrom. Santa Barbara: ABC – CLIO, 2005.

Bibliography

———. *The Industrial Revolution in America: Steam Shipping.* Vol. 3, edited by Kevin Hillstrom. Santa Barbara: ABC–CLIO, 2005.

Hoerr, John P. *And the Wolf Finally Came: The Decline of the American Steel Industry.* Pittsburgh, PA: University of Pittsburgh Press, 1988.

"Internal Combustion Engine." Live Science, https://www.livescience.com/37538-who-invented-the-car.html.

Kalsbeek, L. *Contours of a Christian Philosophy.* Toronto: Wedge, 1975.

Kevles, Daniel J. *In the Name of Eugenics: Genetics and the Uses of Human Heredity.* New York: Alfred A. Knopf, 1985.

Laplace, Pierre-Simon. *A Philosophical Essay on Probabilities.* Translated by Andrew I. Dale. Verlas, NY: Springer, 1995.

Lewis, C.S., *The Lion, the Witch, and the Wardrobe.* New York: Harper Collins, 1978.

Locke, John. *The John Locke Collection.* Karpathos Collections, 2016. Kindle.

Lovejoy, Arthur O. *The Great Chain of Being.* Cambridge, MA: Harvard University Press, 1964.

Mann, Horace. *Life and Works of Horace Mann.* vol. 2. Boston: Lee and Shepard, 1891.

Marsden, George M. *Understanding Fundamentalism and Evangelicalism.* Grand Rapids: Eerdmans, 1991.

Maurer, Armand. "*Scotism and Ockhamism*". *A History of Philosophical Systems*, edited by Vergilius Ferm, 222. New York: The Philosophical Library, 1950.

May, Henry F. *The End of American Innocence: A Study of the First Years of Our Own Time 1912–1917.* Chicago: Quadrangle, 1964.

Miller, Kevin A. "George Whitefield: Did You Know?" *Christianity Today* (1993) http://www.christianitytoday.com/history/issues/issue-38/george-whitefield-did-you-know.html.

Moore, R. I. *The Formation of a Persecuting Society: Power and Deviance in Western Europe, 950–1250.* Oxford: Oxford University Press, 1987.

Morner, Mangus. *Race Mixture in the History of Latin America.* Boston: Little, Brown and Company, 1967.

New York City Government, "New York City Planning." https://www1.nyc.gov/assets/planning/download/pdf/planning-level/nyc-population/historical-population/1790-2000_nyc_foreign_birth_graph.pdf.

"Nominalism." *English Oxford Living Dictionary. https//:en.oxforddictionairies.com/definition/nominalism.* Accessed September, 2017.

"Petroleum Technology History" https://www.greatachievements.org/?id=3677.

Poliakov, Leon. *The History of Anti-Semitism: From Mohammed to the Marranos.* Vol. 2. New York: Vanguard, 1973.

Pruette, Lorine, and G. Stanley Hall. *A Biography of a Mind.* New York: D. Appleton, 1926.

Ramsperger, Albert G. "Early Modern Rationalism." In *A History of Philosophical Systems*, edited by Vergilius Ferm, 243. New York: The Philosophical Library, 1950.

Bibliography

Riessen, H. Van. *The Society of the Future*. Philadelphia: Presbyterian and Reformed, 1952.

Roediger, David R. *Working Toward Whiteness: How America's Immigrants Became White*. New York: Basic, 2005.

Roth, Cecil. *Essential Papers on Judaism and Christianity in Conflict: From Late Antiquity to the Reformation*, edited by Jeremy Cohen. New York: New York University Press, 1991.

Runner, H.E. *Walking in the Way of the Word*. Vol. 1, edited by Kerry Hollingsworth. Grand Rapids: Paideia, 2016.

———. *Walking in the Way of the Word*. Vol 2, edited by Kerry Hollingsworth. Grand Rapids: Paideia, 2009.

Rushdoony, R.J. *The Messianic Character of American Education*. Vallecito: Ross House, 1995.

"The Russian Civil War." *Military History Monthly*. November, 2017.

Schorsch, Jonathan. *Jews and Blacks in the Early Modern World*. Cambridge: Cambridge University Press, 2009.

Schrotenboer, Paul. "Man in God's World." *International Reformed Bulletin* (1967).

Sewell, Keith C. *The Crisis of Evangelical Christianity: Roots, Consequences, and Resolutions*. Eugene, OR: Wipf and Stock, 2016. Kindle.

Singer, Peter. *Hegel: A Very Short Introduction*. Oxford: Oxford University Press, 1983.

Spier, J.M. *An Introduction to Christian Philosophy*. Philipsburg, NJ: Presbyterian and Reformed, 1954.

Sweet, William Warren. *Religion in the Development of American Culture 1765–1840*. Gloucester: Peter Smith, 1963.

Trachtenberg, Joshua. *The Devil and the Jews: The Medieval Conception of the Jew and Its Relation to Modern Antisemitism*. Philadelphia: Jewish Publication Society, 1983.

Troost, Andree. *What Is Reformational Philosophy?* Grand Rapids: Paideia, 2012.

Tornozo, William, ed. *The Fragment: An Incomplete History*. Los Angeles: The Getty Research Institute, 2009.

United States Supreme Court, *Buck v. Bell, Superintendent of State Colony Epileptics and Feeble Minded*. https://www.law.cornell.edu/supremecourt/text/274/200.

Van Reissen, H. *Nietzsche*. Philipsburg, NJ: Presbyterian and Reformed, 1960.

———. *The Society of the Future*. Translated by David Hugh Freeman. Philipsburg, NJ: Presbyterian and Reformed, 1952.

Vander Hoven, John. *Karl Marx*. Toronto: Wedge, 1976.

Vander Stelt, John C. *Philosophy and Scripture: A Study in Old Princeton and Westminster Theology*. Marlton, NJ: Mack, 1978.

Vidal, Gore. *Perpetual War for Perpetual Peace*. New York: Thunder's Mouth, 2002.

Bibliography

Vinci, Leonardo da. *Leonardo's Notebooks: Writing and Art of the Great Master*. Edited by H. Anna Suh. New York: Black Dog and Levanthal, 2005.

Weintraub, J. "Why They Call It the Second City." chicagoreader.com/news-politics/why-they-call-it-the-second-city/.

West, Cornel. *The American Evasion of Philosophy*. Madison, WI: The University of Wisconsin Press, 1989.

Williams, E.I.F. *Horace Mann: Educational Statesman*. New York: Macmillan, 1937.

Winthrop, Hudson, and John Corrigan. *Religion in America*. 5th ed. New York: Macmillan, 1992.

Wolters, Albert M. *Creation Regained: Biblical Basics for a Reformational Worldview*. 2nd edition. Grand Rapids: Eerdmans, 2005.

Wray, Matt. *Not Quite White: White Trash and the Boundaries of Whiteness*. Durham, NC: Duke University Press, 2000.

Wright, N.T. "Cessationism and Why I Pray in Tongues." Youtube, May 31, 2020. https://www.youtube.com/watch?v=slaoT4X-I8o.

Zalta, Edward N., ed. "Substance." *Stanford Encyclopedia of Philosophy*. Last modified November 2018. https://plato.stanford.edu/entries/substance/.

Zuidema, S.U. *Communication and Confrontation*. Toronto: Wedge, 1972.

———. *Kierkegaard*. Philipsburg, NJ: Presbyterian and Reformed, 1960.

———. *Sartre*. Philipsburg, NJ: Presbyterian and Reformed, 1978.

www.ingramcontent.com/pod-product-compliance
Lightning Source LLC
Chambersburg PA
CBHW072152160426
43197CB00012B/2354